A Guide to

Schenkerian Analysis

David Neumeyer
Indiana University

Susan Tepping
Georgia State University

Prentice Hall
Englewood Cliffs, N.J.

Library of Congress Cataloging-in-Publication Data

Neumeyer, David.
    A guide to Schenkerian analysis / David Neumeyer, Susan Tepping.

    Includes bibliographical references and index.
    ISBN 0-13-497215-5
    1. Schenkerian analysis.   I. Tepping, Susan
II. Title.
MT6.N248G8   1992
781--dc20   91-22203
                                                                  CIP
                                                                   MN

Acquisition Editor: Norwell Therien
Editorial Production: Penelope Linskey
Cover Designer: Jayne Conte
Prepress Buyer: Herb Klein
Manufacturing Buyer: Patrice Fraccio

 © 1992 by Prentice-Hall, Inc.
A Simon & Schuster Company
Englewood Cliffs, New Jersey 07632

Printed in the United States of America

10 9 8 7 6 5 4 3 2 1

ISBN 0-13-497215-5

Prentice-Hall International (UK) Limited, *London*
Prentice-Hall of Australia Pty. Limited, *Sydney*
Prentice-Hall Canada Inc., *Toronto*
Prentice-Hall Hispanoamericana, S.A., *Mexico*
Prentice-Hall of India Private Limited, *New Delhi*
Prentice-Hall of Japan, Inc., *Tokyo*
Simon & Schuster Asia Pte. Ltd., *Singapore*
Editora Prentice-Hall do Brasil, Ltda., *Rio de Janeiro*

CONTENTS

PART II: COMPLETE ANALYSES

PREFACE

The object of this book is to support a clear and efficient course of training in Heinrich Schenker's method for analysis of traditional tonal music.

"Traditional tonal music" here means Western art music in the eighteenth and nineteenth centuries, or roughly the period from Bach to Brahms. We do not by any means rule out the possibility or appropriateness of the method (within limits) for analysis of works outside this core of Schenker's musical interests, but such applications form a collection of specialized topics outside the usual scope of study. We have restricted discussion of these topics to Chapter 9, which students and instructor may use or ignore, as they wish.

This manual may be combined with basic reference sources as the material for a complete course, but it is not intended as a substitute for class instruction. Some technical information and certain skills are most efficiently learned by means of a concise text explanation followed by exercises, but Schenkerian analysis must be taught primarily through an instructor and student(s) working out analyses together. We do concentrate on the technical matters (an emphasis very deliberately chosen), but in general we do not attempt to provide complete analytic interpretations, which must go beyond technique to consider artistic, stylistic, or aesthetic problems, since to Schenker, the reason for analysis is the searching-out and grasping of the inner spirit or the inner life of a musical composition, both technically and artistically. This text, therefore, is a resource but not a self-instruction manual nor is it a substitute for selective reading in the scholarly literature.

Furthermore, although we are convinced that they are essential to Schenker's world view and to an understanding and critical assessment of his analytic method, the often radical, sometimes mystical aesthetic, philosophical, religious, and political inflections in his own writings have generally been avoided here for the sake of the most direct possible presentation. The reader will necessarily make—or disregard—connections on his or her own between the analytic tools and their underlying assumptions. Ample opportunity exists through the literature to explore a range of critiques of Schenker's ideas and his method.

One often reads that learning Schenkerian analysis requires "years of practice"—but this shouldn't have to be the case, especially if the method is to be relevant to performance: The musician of normal training ought to have a tool accessible to his or her needs, as we think Schenker in his best moments intended. It does require years of practice to think and speak like a Schenkerian, to fashion intricate discussions of motivic and contrapuntal patterns in a composition, but it does not require such an investment to take direct benefit from certain ideas and insights which link Schenker with many musicians before him as part of the tradition of European music-making.

It is partly for this reason that we begin with an extended study of bass-line sketches (in Part I). The upper parts—that is, everything above the bass—can be surprisingly complex and one can encounter difficulty interpreting them even without the added problem of choosing the appropriate form of the fundamental line. But the bass can be interpreted effectively in terms of a somewhat expanded version of the functional harmonic relationships that all trained musicians know (expanded to include the class of linear or contrapuntal chords). In music of the seventeenth and early eighteenth centuries and again in the nineteenth century, a study of the bass-line alone can be a rewarding analytic exercise. In other words, a reader who stops with Part I can still take away a useful analytic tool.

The same cannot be said for Chapter 4, a very informal introduction to upper-voice analysis which is not especially valuable apart from the chapters that follow it. The reader who desires a study of the upper parts similar in its potential utility to that of the bass analysis chapters here—though much more detailed!—should examine the first six chapters of Forte and Gilbert, *Introduction to Schenkerian Analysis*.

In general, however, our approach to the pedagogy of Schenkerian analysis differs sharply from Forte and Gilbert's. They emphasize reduction, both in analysis and in the organization of their presentation. Thus, their book has two main divisions: the first (Part I or Chapters 1-6) deals entirely with features of the surface of the music, and the second (which encompasses Parts II and III) introduces and expands on what they call "basic axioms," or features of the background and early middlegrounds. The advantage of this approach is that the student is given ample opportunity to practice analysis and achieve insights at or near the familiar level of the score itself. The principal disadvantages are: 1) the student is obliged to make a substantial adjustment in point of view and analytic notation halfway through the book; 2) in Part I, the student is too often confronted with apparently arbitrary readings which depend on middleground or background features from a complete analysis which is not presented until later in the book (if at all); 3) despite Parts II and III, the student is left with an analytic orientation that is contrary to Schenker's own insistence on analysis as re-tracing the path of the composing-out process.

This latter approach, which one might call "generative" rather than reductive, is the one we have followed here. Its disadvantage in the past has been that, in the early stages, it seems almost unbearably abstract, far removed from the practical and immediate concerns with the score that interest most students. Our remedy for this is the bass-line sketch, which allows the student to work quickly and naturally with large-scale formal and tonal design at the same time that he or she learns about the structural levels and analytic notation. Several years' experience with this approach in the classroom has convinced us of its effectiveness.

A difficulty does arise in the relationship of background and middleground models to traditional formal design categories.

Schenker's theory of form, as presented in Part III, Chapter 5, of *Free Composition* is entirely dependent on his theory of the *Ursatz* (or fundamental structure) and composing-out (the structural levels). For him, traditional formal designs are the surface result of underlying tonal events. He divides forms into one to five-part designs depending on the tonal features of the first middleground (*1. Schicht*), such as interruption and deep-level neighbor notes. Thus, the essential features of form (like those of rhythm and meter) arise in the first middleground level, even though a two-part form at that level might resolve itself into a Bach dance, a Beethoven sonata movement, or a Chopin nocturne in the foreground.

Although this concept of form is a logical outcome of the theory of the fundamental structure, it is internally inconsistent and sometimes confusing (though this may be due to the fact that the chapter is more like an outline than a full exposition of the topic). We have found it more satisfying and effective from all standpoints, musical, historical, and pedagogical, essentially to equate the structural significance of formal and tonal design. Thus, Chapters 3 and 8 discuss at some length paradigms for the interaction of some stereotyped form genres of the seventeenth to nineteenth centuries with the *Ursatz* forms and first or second middleground structures. The equating of formal and tonal design, furthermore, is necessary for a pedagogically adequate introduction to the bass-line sketch; that is, positioning of the background—and often early middleground—tones depends to a great extent on an assessment of large-scale form. By forcing the student to consider large-scale articulations of a piece first, along with the ways in which the structures of the background and first middleground relate to them, this method keeps the focus on the composing-out process, or on "generative form," which is not only correct from Schenker's standpoint but also helps to make the analysis work more efficient and reliable.

Instructors will be aware that the first co-author has written several articles proposing revisions of some structures of the background and early middleground. These articles and ideas derived from them have been entirely excluded from Chapters 1-8 (even where statements here conflict with conclusions drawn there). We have done this in order to simplify the presentation and to ensure that this book will be usable by a broader audience. The first co-author remains confident that these revisions and similar ideas will continue to receive serious consideration by those who have an interest in the development and future of Schenkerian analysis as a scholarly discipline. A part of the text of Chapter 9 comes from the following article by the first co-author: "Fragile Octaves, Broken Lines: On Some Limitations in Schenkerian Theory and Practice," *In Theory Only* 11/3 (1989): 11-30. Reproduced by permission of the Michigan Music Theory Society.

The notational style of Schenkerian graphs can vary widely; Schenker himself did not seem to promote a strictly systematized graphing style—the closest he might be said to have come is in *Five Graphic Music Analyses*. In the United States, there are two main styles, the first used and taught by the more conservative Schenker students (Oswald Jonas and Hans Weisse) and in turn by their students and associates, prominent among them Ernst Oster, Allen Forte, David Beach, and John Rothgeb; the second being Felix Salzer's, as presented in *Structural Hearing* (also the notational style of the journal *Music Forum*). Among Salzer's many students and associates who use this graphing method are Saul Novack and Roy Travis.

The style used in this manual is based on the style the first co-author learned from Allen Forte in the early 1970's (quite different from what is taught in Forte and Gilbert). A number of changes have been induced by the needs of the bass-line sketches and by the influence of the distinct manner of another Schenker student, the late Felix-Eberhard von Cube, whose *Book of the Musical Artwork* was recently published. Three of Cube's analyses are reproduced in the Exercises for Part II.

For harmonic analysis, Schenker used the Roman numeral labels of the Viennese *Stufentheorie*, an expansion of Rameauian harmonic theory which originated with Simon Sechter in the first half of the nineteenth century. Only upper-case numerals are employed, inver-

sions are not indicated (thus, no figured-bass symbols are added), and alterations are shown with accidentals to the right of the numeral. Thus, "I" is the tonic in both major and minor modes; "II" may indicate a diminished or a minor triad on the second degree of a minor key; and "III♯" would be a major triad on the third degree of a major key.

Since the labels of *Stufentheorie* are little used in the United States, we have not hesitated to change to the far more common labelling system derived ultimately from Gottfried Weber and E. F. R. Richter, but more directly from Percy Goetschius and Walter Piston. Chord quality is shown by upper and lower case, inversion by added figured-bass symbols. Thus, "I" is the tonic in major, but "i" is the tonic in minor; "v" is the minor dominant, "V" the major dominant; "ii^0" is a diminished triad, "III$^+$" is an augmented triad; "I^6" is the tonic triad, first inversion; "V$^4_3$" the dominant seventh, second inversion; and so on. The reader is warned that in many cases the chord labels are applied only to structural or prolonged harmonies and the inversion of the first or subsequent presentations of a chord are often not shown (especially in middleground graphs).

We have, however, retained the "great/small" method of designating specific pitches: c' = middle C; a' = the A above middle C; c'' = the C above middle C; small c = the C below middle C; great C = the C two octaves below middle C; and so on. When letter-names are used but the specific octave position is not important to the point, we use capital letters, as "C." To make sure the difference is clear, references to notes in the great or small octaves will always include the prefix "great" or "small."

This text is designed for upper-level undergraduates and graduate students. Students should have had at least two years of traditional college theory training, particularly in harmony—and preferably Schenker-oriented (from the most recent editions of books such as Aldwell and Schachter, *Harmony and Voice-Leading*; Allen Forte, *Tonal Harmony in Concept and Practice*; or Joel Lester, *Harmony in Tonal*

Music), or else based on a clearly presented hierarchical view of harmony and form (as in Allen Winold, *Harmony: Patterns and Principles*). A hierarchical understanding of tonal function will also be developed through the study of bass-line sketches in Part I below. Some study of form and analysis and sixteenth-century (or species) counterpoint, likewise, would be helpful but is not required. (The study of strict counterpoint is a must for anyone who wishes to do advanced work in Schenkerian analysis.) An integrated textbook such as Leo Kraft's *Gradus* would also serve as preparation, though we will use a more limited stylistic base here.

Although it is possible, it is not especially desirable to use this manual independently of other sources. The reader should have available as references at least the following works:

1. Heinrich Schenker, *Free Composition*, trans. and ed. Ernst Oster (New York 1979).

2. Heinrich Schenker, *Five Graphic Music Analyses* (New York 1932; repr. 1969).

3. Felix Salzer, *Structural Hearing* (New York 1952; reprint ed. 1962).

4. Allen Forte and Steven Gilbert, *Introduction to Schenkerian Analysis* (New York 1982). References below are to: "Forte and Gilbert."

5. Felix Eberhard von Cube, *The Book of the Musical Artwork*, trans. and ed. by David Neumeyer, George R. Boyd, and Scott Harris (Lewiston NY 1988). References below are to the title or to: "Cube."

Exercises are collected in groups at the ends of Parts I and II. References are included at appropriate points in the chapters using the format [EXERCISE I.1]. We should emphasize that these are only suggestions; the instructor should feel free to choose and order exercises according to class needs.

Our thanks to Edilberto Cuellar, Raymond Foster, Roger Hudson, Rick Littlefield, Ronald Rodman, and Steve Sherrill, students in graduate analysis seminars at Indiana and Georgia State Universities, who used the second and third drafts and helped locate errors and inconsistencies; to Edilberto Cuellar, who assisted in copying graphics onto the computer; to Janice Hunton, who several years ago helped clarify the analyzed-bass notation in connection with a failed textbook project, and one of whose analyses is included in the samples; to Marianne Kielian-Gilbert, who pointed out a number of errors of detail in the analysis graphs and whose insistence on the bass-line sketch in her undergraduate class in nineteenth-century music has helped to reinforce our belief in its value as a pedagogical tool; to Eric Lai, who pointed out several typographical errors in the third draft; to Nicol Viljoen, whose careful reading of both first and second drafts has resulted in a number of improvements and whose analyses of Chopin mazurkas we have drawn upon for three examples in Chapter 6; and to Allen Winold, for his critical reading of the opening chapters. Our thanks also to two anonymous Prentice-Hall reviewers, who offered useful and practical suggestions, many of which have been adopted here.

The present book evolved from a typewritten original by the first co-author in 1982 through three further drafts, each of which involved extensive revision based on the co-authors' classroom experience and, in the last case, readers' reports. The final version was produced using the Apple Macintosh with PageMaker, Microsoft Word, Superpaint, Professional Composer, and NoteWriter. Camera-ready copy was generated on an Apple LaserWriter using high-resolution paper. The main text font is Palatino 10, with Bookman for titles and boldface and a specially edited font for accidentals, careted numbers, and figured bass symbols.

The Authors
Bloomington, Indiana
Atlanta, Georgia

INTRODUCTION

The music theory and associated analytic method of the Viennese pianist and music theorist Heinrich Schenker (1868-1935) was developed in order to reveal the secrets of organic coherence in the works of, primarily, the Viennese masters of the eighteenth and nineteenth centuries. Schenker's theory is unique in its heavy emphasis on counterpoint or voice leading and in its system of structural levels. The particular strengths of the analytic method are its ability to interpret and represent counterpoint or voice leading on a broad scale, to connect this voice-leading motion systematically to harmony, and to integrate these with an expanded concept of motivic development (and, if one allows for some problems in the formulations, with concepts of form and of rhythm and meter as well).

Schenker's theory has (at least) the following bases or components: it is *natural theory* (based on the overtone series or the "chord of nature"); it is based on *organic unity* (a biological analogy); it uses *diatonic harmonic functions* as a paradigm (chromaticism is elaboration or distortion); it uses *species counterpoint* as a paradigm, of which free composition is an elaboration; it has a strong *ideological* slant with cultural, political, and religious elements (generally, German chauvinism, nineteenth-century aesthetic culture, and political reaction—in the immediate context of post-World War I); and it assumes that only the *genius* is a true musician and artist.

To Schenker, the genius "improvises" on the basis of the nature-given elements and the natural systems of harmony and counterpoint: this is **"composing-out" (Auskomponierung)** from the background.[1] Through a series of increasingly free, more detailed **levels (Schichten)**, we reach the actual score, with all its details. Schenker believed the genius could grasp and control all the levels simultaneously, but the non-genius was condemned to flounder about in the foreground, creating pastiches rather than organically coherent musical artworks: "Composing-out *is* music. History demonstrates this in the works of the great masters; and history will also show that it is the loss of ability to compose-out that has been music's downfall…

Thus, the whole of the foreground is a single, surpassing diminution, a single figure."[2]

The core progression or fundamental structure (**Ursatz**) from which the composer begins represents the most basic and natural aspects of harmony, melody, and counterpoint. He develops a complete work by composing through a series of levels, adding successive layers of elaborating lines and harmonies (**diminutions**) as **prolongations** of the background elements until the most elaborate level—the score itself—is reached (see Table 1). The three main levels in this process are **background, middleground, and foreground**. The middleground and foreground (but especially the former) may be subdivided into further levels as well. The object of analysis, then, is to re-trace this path of composing-out to allow musicians of understanding an appreciation of the methods of the masters, as well to suggest how their work differs from the pastiches of lesser composers. Such an appreciation of the inner life of masterworks would then be the surest guide to both listening and performance.

The object of the narrative below is to follow the path of the composing-out process, using as an example an excerpt from Act II of Carl Maria von Weber's famous romantic opera *Der Freischütz*.

---

[1]Throughout this introduction, important terms are given in bold-face in the first reference to them. The English translations in most cases follow Appendix 5 in *Free Composition*, pp. 163-164), rather than the more limited glossary that appears in *Five Graphic Music Analyses*, pp. 23-24.

[2]Schenker, *Das Meisterwerk in der Musik*, vol. 2, p. 40. On improvising from the background, see another essay from volume 2 of *Meisterwerk*: "Organic Structure and Sonata Form," trans. Orin Grossman, in Maury Yeston, ed., *Readings in Schenker Analysis and Other Approaches*, pp. 38-53. This is one of Schenker's best (and most entertainingly polemical) presentations of some of the essential ideas in his theory.

TABLE 1. Composing-out and related concepts

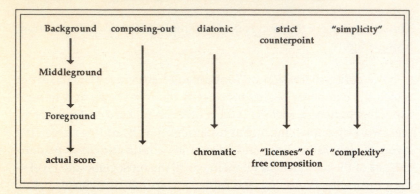

Background	composing-out	diatonic	strict counterpoint	"simplicity"
↓				
Middleground				
↓				
Foreground				
↓	↓	↓	↓	↓
actual score		chromatic	"licenses" of free composition	"complexity"

The overtone series of Ex. 0.1a generates the E-major triad of Ex. 0.1b. (Schenker, like most theorists up to his time, rejected the seventh and ninth partials for his system—here, D♮ and F♯.) The primordial compositional decision, so to speak, is the revoicing of this chord. In this case, the fifth (5̂) is placed in the soprano (Ex. 0.1c). This creates the work's **tonal space** (Tonraum), which is strictly speaking the beginning of the background (Exs. 0.1a and b are part of the systemic "pre-background"). The deepest compositional task is to carry this 5̂ by step down to the 1̂ (to its "rest" in the fundamental, as it were): Ex. 0.1d. The **fundamental line** (Urlinie) created by this descent also requires harmonization. There are a number of ways to accomplish this, some "stronger" than others; the version used in this piece is shown in Example 0.2. [The fundamental line may begin from 5̂ or from 3̂, occasionally from 8̂, but always moves down to 1̂ by diatonic step.]

EXAMPLE 0.1 The overtone series on E, tonal space, and the fundamental line (*Urlinie*)

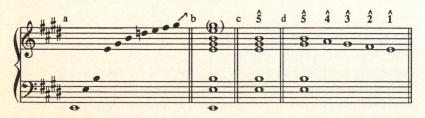

The motion of the bass in Ex. 0.2 is already a slight elaboration of the essential harmonic motion, I-V-I. This I-V-I pattern is called the **"bass arpeggiation"** (Bassbrechung). In this case, great A supports a dominant preparation chord, ii⁶. The **Urlinie** and **Bassbrechung** together form the **Ursatz**, or **fundamental structure**. The Urlinie represents the essence of melody (diatonic line), the Bassbrechung the essence of harmony (the tonic-dominant relationship), and the two in combination the essence of counterpoint (first-species consonances). The most common stereotype of the harmonic phrase consists of the tonic, tonic extension or **prolongation** (by some means), plus a close (cadence). Ex. 0.3 shows one of the simplest prolongations of the tonic: a nested I-V-I pattern. [In the various I-V-I patterns, the V is called a **dividing dominant** (Teiler).]

EXAMPLE 0.2 The fundamental structure (*Ursatz*)

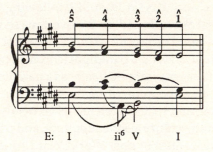

E: I   ii⁶ V   I

EXAMPLE 0.3 Prolongation using nested I-V-I

E: I   ii⁶ V   I

Ex. 0.4 adds further details (diminutions or embellishing figures): prolongation of $\hat{5}$ over V with a neighbor note (c#''), a dividing secondary or applied dominant (V^7/V), and simple repetition of V; also, revoicing of inner parts in the second tonic chord (simple arpeggiation as composing-out or prolongation).

Note: Strictly speaking, prolongation refers to the expansion of species counterpoint, but this sense has been mostly lost in the Schenker literature, where prolongation is synonymous with composing-out in the middleground and foreground. Another note: Don't worry if you don't understand the placement or meaning of every symbol in this or the following graphs—we will learn about them starting in Chapter 1. What is important now is to grasp the general principles of fundamental structure and composing-out through structural levels.

Ex. 0.5 adds still more figuration to $\hat{5}$ over I: an embellishing diminished seventh chord (a linear chord created by neighbor notes) and a third-line in the soprano (the beamed notes B-A-G#). This line is harmonized by another I-V-I progression, or yet another nesting, since this I-V-I occurs inside the middleground I-V-I added in Ex. 0.3. Another new feature is an upper third-line above the $\hat{5}$ over V. **Line (Zug)** refers to a figure formed by stepwise motion through a consonant interval. Thus, a third-line covers the interval of the third (a minor third, B down to G#, in the first case, a major third, D# down to B in the second). (The fundamental line of this piece is itself an example of a fifth-line.) An "upper third-line" is an embellishing figure which starts above the main note of the melody (here, B) and comes down to it. Activity above the main melody note is referred to generically as **boundary play (Ränderspiel)**.

The final example (Ex. 0.6) includes another level of composing-out in its first system, a chordal reduction of the score in its second system;[3] and a piano/vocal reduction of the score itself at the bottom. The latter is not the entire scene-and-aria sung by Agathe, but only the first strophe of its hymn-like first part; this is treated as if it were a complete composition only for the purposes of this demonstration.

EXAMPLES 0.4 and 0.5 Further prolongations, particularly of V (0.4) and of I (0.5)

In Ex. 0.6, the first tonic chord is revoiced in the upper parts; this forms an **initial ascent (Anstieg)** to the structural $\hat{5}$. (Note: Strictly speaking, inital ascent refers to stepwise ascent to the first note of the fundamental line, but the term is generally used to refer to a prefix made up of a line, tonic-triad arpeggiation, or a combination of both.) Further elaboration of the dominant extension occurs in bars 5-8: a quick V-V/V-V (=B: I-V-I) progression in bars 5-6 with an ascending third-line, and in bar 6 a prefix to the dominant, which creates an escape tone in the soprano. The repetition of the tonic (bars 9 ff.) is now also elaborated with simple dividing dominants. In bar 13, there is a **register transfer**; that is, a note in a continuing voice is shifted an

---

[3] A chordal reduction is essentially the score itself with non-harmonic tones removed. "Rhythmic reduction," which means the same thing, is the term used by Forte and Gilbert.

octave away (e′ to e′′), moving above the true soprano note b′.

The $\hat{4}$ of the fundamental line (bar 14) is not actually reached by the soprano, but by what is literally the alto (which moves b′-a′ in bars 13-14). This confusion of voices arises because of the register transfer, in which the "literal" soprano takes a note which "actually" belongs to the alto of the underlying voice leading. The soprano itself does reach a′ on beat 2 but the $\hat{3}$ (bar 15) does not sound at all, except as a grace note to the F$\sharp$. Nevertheless, from the earlier levels of the composing-out, we can tell that the note g$\sharp$′ is plainly implied here—that is, required by the underlying voice leading. Such displacement of structural tones at later levels is not uncommon. Finally, the harmonization of the $\hat{3}$ and $\hat{2}$ with a cadential dominant figure is acceptable, one of a very few exceptions to the general rule that notes of the fundamental line require consonant harmonic support. [The cadential dominant figure is explained in Chapter 1 below, under the heading "Expansion of the Harmonic Cycle through Inversions."]

The content of foreground, middleground, and background—the three levels of structure Schenker names—is not precisely prescribed, but in general we can follow the rule of thumb that the levels of composing-out up to the fundamental structure (the fundamental line plus the bass arpeggiation) are "pre-background" and the fundamental structure itself is background; that there are several intermediate levels of middleground; and that the level closest to the surface is foreground. In our analysis, Examples 0.1-0.2 are "pre-background" and background, 0.3-0.5 are middleground (they might be labelled middleground 1, 2, and 3), and Example 0.6 is foreground.

Since Schenker talks about three broad levels of activity—background, middleground, and foreground—it is usually assumed that analyses should have three levels corresponding to these. In fact, this is often not the case. The number of levels may vary according to the complexity of the piece or according to what the analyst wishes to show, and these levels may be distributed in differing ways. A common procedure is to show one background, two or more middlegrounds, and one or, very occasionally, two foregrounds. *Five Graphic Music Analyses* may serve as our model: only one of the analyses has three levels which correspond nicely to background, middleground, and foreground (*Well-Tempered Clavier*, Vol. 1, C Major Prelude). Three consist of a background (fundamental line and bass arpeggiation), three numbered middlegrounds (labelled *Schichten*), and an *Urlinietafel*, which is a special type of foreground graph. The *Urlinietafel*, for which we will use the non-literal translation "score foreground," is essentially a foreground graph with barlines and surface motivic figures or other literal score features shown. (The fifth analysis in *Five Graphic Music Analyses* is not complete; it shows only the development section of Haydn, Sonata in E$\flat$ Major, Hob. XVI/49, first movement—essentially three levels of foreground.)

ADDITIONAL READING:

Perhaps the clearest guide to the structural levels and sublevels, their number, and typical contents are the *Five Graphic Music Analyses*; equally good are the many analyses in *The Book of the Musical Artwork*. Among other sources, you might consult the following:

1. In Appendix II to the translation of Schenker's *Harmony*, Oswald Jonas presents an analytical narrative similar to the one above; his subject is J. S. Bach, Little Prelude in F Major.

2. Jonas also gives a concise outline of Schenker's basic theoretical system (the role of the overtone series, the primacy of the perfect fifth, "natural" and "artifical" systems, key, scale, and so on) in his *Introduction to the Theory of Heinrich Schenker*, Chapter 1. His engaging, less technical discussion of the fundamental structure appears in Chapter 4 of the same book.

3. Forte and Gilbert discuss the same topic in a clear, readable fashion in their Chapter 7, though they begin with the unfortunate statement that the background is the level "which often seemed to concern [Schenker] least" (131).

4. See also Nicholas Cook, *A Guide to Musical Analysis* (New York 1987), 27-66; and Jonathan Dunsby and Arnold Whittall, *Music Analysis in Theory and Practice* (New Haven 1988), 29-52. Both are general introductions to Schenker's analytic system; both offer commentary on readings from *Five Graphic Music Analyses*.

EXAMPLE 0.6 "Leise, leise, fromme Weise," foreground, chordal reduction, and piano score

Lightly, lightly, pious tune,
Wing your way to the starry sky!
Song, resound, solemnly bear
My prayer to Heaven's door!

5

PART I: ANALYZED BASS NOTATION

Chapter 1: Summary of Analyzed Bass Notation

We will not attempt to deal with all components of a composition immediately. Instead, we will start with the bass, which can be organized and interpreted for the most part according to the harmonic functions familiar to all trained musicians. These bass-line sketches will sometimes require adjustments when used for complete analyses later on, but such adjustments are usually few and are mostly matters of notational details relating to the structural hierarchies of composing-out, or else they result from the occasional overriding of functional relationships by contrapuntal figures. If the notation used here has any apparently arbitrary qualities, that is because it is designed in such a way as to minimize changes that might be necessary later on.

The upper parts (all those above the bass) will sometimes be mentioned, but they are normally much more complex and, in any case, require the bass to aid in their interpretation. Chapter 4 contains an informal introduction to upper-voice analysis. Even when we attempt complete, formally constructed analysis graphs involving all components of a piece (in Chapters 5 and following), we will often find it to our advantage to begin by working out a bass-line sketch.

This chapter consists primarily of a tabular summary of the conversion of functional patterns into an analyzed bass notation which can be used essentially without modification as a component of complete analyses in Part II. Some guidelines for the application of this notation, in the form of brief narratives of four analyses, are given in Chapter 2. Beyond their use as demonstrations, these narratives are intended to show that, independently of the full apparatus of Schenkerian analysis, the bass-line sketch can be a powerful and very useful analytic tool. For many practical applications, the bass-line itself, interpreted in Schenkerian graphic notation, can be sufficient. If desired, or to aid in the clearest possible presentation, one may add figured-bass symbols, Roman numerals, or other symbols showing chord quality, position, or harmonic function.

TONIC AND DOMINANT PATTERNS

Differentiation of functional levels is shown by the manner in which pitches are notated:

"Open notes" are those of deepest structural importance (background or first middleground).

Stemmed closed notes are of lesser importance (middleground or foreground).

Unstemmed closed notes are subordinate (foreground only).

Harmonic progressions are grouped together either by beams (at earlier levels of structure) or by slurs (at later levels). The first line of Ex. 1.1 shows several I-V-I patterns, in order from the deepest structural level to the foreground. The second line shows a series of embedded I-V-I patterns. The first note, the open C, is a background note which is prolonged or embellished by two I-V-I groups, the "deeper" (and longer-range) one shown with stemmed and slurred closed notes, the "shallower" (and more immediate) shown with slurred but unstemmed closed notes. It is very important for an understanding of the notation of graphs (and of the relationship of prolongation and structural levels, for that matter) to recognize that the initial C functions as the first note of a I-V-I group at all three levels. The general principle is that a note which belongs to one level is active at all later levels. Thus, the first C belongs to the background but initiates—and is part of—each of the two embellishing functional groups.

In order to illustrate the nesting of I-V-I patterns, an excerpt from one of Kuhnau's Biblical Sonatas is treated in Ex. 1.2 as if it were a complete piece, with a framework of open notes. The formal

EXAMPLE 1.1 I-V-I patterns

EXAMPLE 1.2 Johann Kuhnau, Biblical Sonata "David and Goliath," Dance of the People, bars 1-8

hierarchy of phrase and period affects the nestings used: bars 1-5 are given as a I-V-I pattern with stemmed closed notes, because they are associated with harmonic progression across the phrase, but bars 5-7 are treated as subordinate (unstemmed closed notes). This small-level interaction between the tonal and voice-leading structure and formal design is a preview of considerations that will remain a constant factor throughout our work with bass-line sketches (and beyond).

The patterns of I-V-I motion are further illustrated in Example 1.3, a Schubert waltz. The bass-line sketch in the upper staff is a foreground reading which is reduced to a middleground reading in the lower staff. Left-hand notes on the afterbeats (beats 2 and 3) are not included in the sketch; this is generally true of analyses of such dances, so long as there is no chord change within the bar. The figure in bars 9-12 is discussed in the next section.

As the commentary for Example 1.3 has already suggested, the hierarchy of I-V-I patterns in most compositions will depend on formal design (variants or exceptions derive from special linear patterns of the upper voices). In the case of Ex. 1.3, it is one of the

patterns for dance forms discussed in Chapter 3 below, the "binary/ternary" form, a very common design in dances from the later eighteenth and early nineteenth centuries in which the first part ends on I, the second introduces and prolongs the first background V, and the reprise (bar 17) closes the first background group and contains all of the second.

In *Five Graphic Music Analyses*, graphs of certain structural levels show I-V-I groupings with "whole notes"; that is, unstemmed open notes slurred together but not beamed. See, for example, the *Ursatz* (background) for the J. S. Bach setting of the chorale "Ich bin's, ich sollte büssen." This notation is acceptable only for the background, and thus only for the primary structural bass arpeggiation(s). This "whole note" graphing style can also be found in *Free Composition* (see, for instance, Figs. 7,a (Beethoven); 7,b (Chopin); 30,a (Chopin)) but Schenkerian analysts today rarely use it. In many other figures, Schenker uses the beamed open-note groups of our Ex. 1.1—as in Figs. 14 through 19 (models); 20,4 (Mozart); etc.

In the *1. Schicht* (Middleground 1) of the same chorale analysis, the bass tones are shown as "half notes"—stemmed open notes—

EXAMPLE 1.3 Schubert, *Valses sentimentales*, D. 779, no. 3

slurred but not beamed together. (This is true of the other analyses in the collection, as well.) In *Free Composition*, Schenker uses beamed and slurred open-note groups interchangeably. For your own work, prefer the beamed groups of Ex. 1.1. The beamed tonic tones in the second and third middlegrounds of the chorale analysis, by the way, are anomalies—don't use them as models.

[EXERCISE I.15]

EXPANSION OF I-V-I THROUGH USE OF PRE-DOMINANT HARMONY

Tonic and dominant patterns can be expanded by the insertion of a pre-dominant, resulting most often in progressions such as I-IV-V-I or I-ii-V-I (generalized functions: tonic-subdominant-dominant-tonic or T-(S)-D-T), as shown in Ex. 1.4.

EXAMPLE 1.4 I-IV (ii)-V-I patterns

In the first model (Ex. 1.4a), the chord above F could be either C: I or ii^6—the notation remains the same in either case. The interlocking slurs are a special notation convention which you should use whenever possible. The second model is an alternative to the first: the flagged note simply draws more attention to the complete harmonic cycle. You may use the first and second models interchangeably. The third model shows the notation when ii, rather than ii^6, is used—a flagged note could be used here, instead. (In *Free Composition*, Figures 15, 16, and 18, Schenker actually uses a flagged *open* note, but in almost all the subsequent analytic graphs, the flagged note is closed.)

The final two models (Exs. 1.4d and e) give two versions of the same reading: the first is preferred, but the second is acceptable, especially if it helps avoid visual clutter in the graph (due to too many slurs and beams arising from the first I).

In Ex. 1.5, the opening of a Haydn Menuet, lower-level I-V-I figures in bars 1-3 embellish the I of the T-(S)-D-T cycle. Such prolongation of the first tonic is a stereotype of much traditional tonal music. The same procedure is used in the Weber example discussed in the Introduction above: there, several subordinate I-V-I figures expand the first tonic of a I-ii^6-V-I progression (first shown in Examples 0.2 and 0.3). Also, look again at Ex. 1.3 above (Schubert). The progression G: I-V/V-V (bars 1, 9, 10) was notated in the same way as a diatonic progression with those bass notes (that is, I-ii-V). This is characteristic of Schenkerian treatment of chromaticism: chromatic sonorities are understood as alterations of, or substitutions for, diatonic chords.

EXAMPLE 1.5 Haydn, Sonata in C, Hob. XVI/1, Menuet, bars 1-4

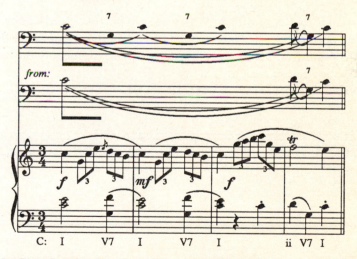

In *Five Graphic Music Analyses*, the first middleground for the Bach chorale shows the typical notation of a full harmonic cycle, including the interlocking slurs for I-IV-V. See also the first middleground for the Prelude in C Major; third middleground for Chopin, Etude in F Major, three instances in bars 1-75; second and third middlegrounds, Etude in C Minor, end. The second middleground of the F-Major Etude also appears in *Free Composition*, Fig. 7,b, with slightly different contents, including a renotated harmonic cycle in bars 61-95.

Note on terminology: The function we have described as "S" or "subdominant" does not have a specific label in Schenker's theory. He refers only to a "contrapuntal-melodic step of a second" (*Free Composition*, p. 30), a label too cumbersome for us to use here. The label "S," however, implies too fixed a harmonic orientation, and we will therefore use the terms "prefix to the dominant" or "pre-domi-nant" to refer to IV, ii, or their functional relatives or chromatic variants (including V/V) when they are part of this motion toward a dominant in a controlling I-V-I framework.

[EXERCISE I.4]

EXPANSION OF I-V-I THROUGH ARPEGGIATION

The span from I ascending to V may be split into two thirds, generating the harmonic patterns, I-iii-V or I-III -V; in the minor key, i-III-v or i-III-V (see Exs. 1.6a and b).[1] The last of these is probably the most

EXAMPLE 1.6 Patterns with iii or III.

C: I iii V I   c: i III V i   c: i III (ii°⁶) V i   c: i III ii°⁶ V i
   (III)   (Vᵇ-♮)

---

[1]Our notation of these models differs slightly from Schenker's in *Free Composition*, Figs. 14 through 16, in that we leave off the flag from the mediant. You may use either form.

common. Ex. 1.7 reads a typical progression from the opening of a Chopin Mazurka. When a passing tone is placed between the third and fifth degrees, confusion can arise over the interpretation—see the alternatives in Exs. 1.6c and d. In the first case, the III as "third-divider" has priority and $\hat{4}$ is simply a passing tone (even if it supports a chord); in the second case, the III is a prolongation of the tonic but the primary progression is the harmonic cycle, i-ii°⁶-V-i. Schenker says a correct reading relies on the upper parts: "The filling-in [from $\hat{3}$ to $\hat{5}$] can also take on other meanings, depending on the position of the tones of the fundamental line" (*Free Composition*, 30). For our purposes now, the best choice is a matter of context: if the III is so prominent in the composition that reducing it to a "mere" elaboration of the tonic would seem to distort the music, then use the model of Ex. 1.6c; otherwise, favor Ex. 1.6d.

In *Five Graphic Music Analyses*, Chopin F-Major Etude, the levels from the second middleground on, bars 1-61, show an overall harmonic motion I-III#³-V⁷-I (see Ex. 1.8 for a summary of this progression). We should also comment on the dotted slurs which appear in the bass in this passage in Schenker's reading and which may be found in all the analyses in that collection (occasionally in *Free Composition*, as well). Schenker uses the dotted slur to emphasize recurrence of a tone or its transfer to another octave, rather than some functional group in which the tone and its recurrence are the first and last members. In this Etude, the long dotted slur in the bass from F in

EXAMPLE 1.8 Chopin, Etude in F Major, op. 10, no. 8, summary of progression in bars 1-61

F: I   III   V   I

bar 1 to F in bar 61 draws attention to the return of F, independently of the functional group I-III#3-V7-I, which is indicated by the solid slur above it. In the Bach chorale analysis, dotted slurs are used to show bass couplings (which we may describe informally as structurally significant octave transfers) but recurrent tones in the soprano. You may regard the dotted slur as an optional symbol, to be employed if it will improve the clarity of the graph or bring out significant recurrences or register transfers.

EXAMPLE 1.7 Chopin, Mazurka in G Minor, op. 67, no. 2, bars 1-6

EXPANSION OF THE HARMONIC CYCLE THROUGH INVERSIONS

The use of chord inversions in I-V-I motions or in the complete harmonic cycle results in arpeggiations, lines, and neighbor notes, as illustrated in Ex. 1.9. In the fourth model (Ex. 1.9d), there is no slur between the second and third notes (scale degrees $\hat{3}$ and $\hat{4}$). This notation avoids any chance of confusing the primary functional relationships: I and I⁶ are a group, but I-IV (or ii⁶)-V-I are another, distinct group (and at a different structural level, too). If it is necessary to bring out the third-line $\hat{3}$-$\hat{4}$-$\hat{5}$, it is best to remove the stem from $\hat{4}$ and the cross-slurs, as in Ex. 1.9e. The interpretation you pick depends on the individual composition, but for our purposes now, give priority to the functional relationships and notate as in Ex. 1.9d. (All this, of course, is very similar to the advice given in the previous section for identical bass patterns involving III rather than I⁶.)

EXAMPLE 1.9 Expansion of the harmonic cycle

Interlocking slurs are not used for Ex.1.9k, even though the underlying functional progression is I-IV-V-I (precisely, I-IV⁶-V⁶-I). The reason is that this type of passage emphasizes the melodic quality of the bass motion rather than the harmonic or functional one. This situation also reflects the ambivalence of the bass and its progressions: it is the carrier of harmony but it is also a voice in the voice leading and thus can create melodic figures in the same way as other voices. Learning to distinguish between these different uses is excellent preparation for work on complete analyses (that is, analyses of all the parts).

11

In Ex. 1.10, the first tonic harmony is prolonged by a subordinate functional cycle (I-ii$^4_2$-V$^{6-7}_5$-I), then another cycle is used for the cadence. In bars 1-5, the bass might be understood either as a I-V-I bass arpeggiation or as a neighbor motion G-F♯-G. (The special symbol used in bar 5—unfolding—is explained in a section near the end of this chapter.) Note that in the cadence the chord usually labelled as I$^6_4$ appears. Schenker understands this chord as part of a "cadential dominant" figure, thus not a tonic chord at all but a dominant with double embellishment by 6-5 and 4-3—so: V$^{6-5}_{4-3}$, not I$^6_4$-V. (The figured-bass symbols should go *above* the V; this is a convention, but it helps to avoid misreading as a V$^6_4$; that is, a second inversion of the dominant triad.) The "cadential dominant" is perhaps the most important of the class of "contrapuntal chords"; that is, chords in which the melodic functions overwhelm and cancel out any possible harmonic function—two other common instances are IV$^6_4$ in the progression I-IV$^6_4$-I and the actual V$^6_4$ in the progression I-V$^6_4$-I^6.

Second inversion major or minor triads, then, are used as passing chords (as in I-V$^6_4$-I^6), as auxiliary or neighboring chords (as in I-IV$^6_4$-I), as part of a chordal arpeggiation (as in I-I^6-I$^6_4$-I), or as part of a cadential dominant figure. Only very rarely will a second inversion triad act as a harmonically functioning chord.

The first tonic in Ex. 1.11 is prolonged by means of a simple I-V-I, followed by a neighbor note (supporting V^6), then a change of bass to I^6. In section B, V is embellished by V^6. The bass notation follows the model of the "binary-ternary" form. Note that the structural dominant is shown as arriving at the end of B, not the beginning, even though there is a dominant at that point also (bar 9). The reason is that the dominant at bar 9 is not decisively established—it is still easier to hear the dominant of bars 9-10 resolving to the tonic of bar 11 than it is to hear the reverse, the tonic of bar 11 embellishing the dominant.

EXAMPLE 1.10 Beethoven, Sonata, op. 14, no. 2, I, bars 1-7

EXAMPLE 1.11 Mozart, Symphony No. 35, III, Trio

EXAMPLE 1.12 Haydn, Sonata in C, Hob. XVI/1, Menuet

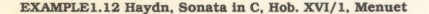

Phrase structure seems to support (perhaps even create) this hearing: the four-bar phrase from 9-12 ends on the tonic, not the dominant. It is the next four-bar phrase that reaches the dominant at the end. The pedal point that extends this dominant (bars 16-19) is represented in the lower level with two notes slurred—these are the first and last notes, or E in bar 16 and in bar 19.

This example also introduces an alternative notational device: differing stem lengths to show hierarchy, especially in the I-V-I bass arpeggiations. These are not required but are sometimes useful in more complex contexts, if you exhaust other ways to show distinctions of level.

Ex. 1.12 gives all of the Haydn Menuet introduced in Ex. 1.5 above. In section A, bars 5-8, the motion is through the octave, outlining the tonic triad (C-G-E-C), although the last C is displaced from small c to c'. In the parallel phrase of section B2 (bars 17-20), the progression is altered to a form identical to the sixth model above.

Compare the beginning of section B here with the corresponding place in Ex. 1.11. In the latter, the structural dominant arrives late and the tonic retains its functional role to that point. In Ex. 1.12, on the other hand, the structural dominant appears at the end of A, and thus B acts as foreground prolongation of it. The I^6 in bar 9 is not a true tonic harmony but an embellishment of the dominant, as the notation shows (the note small e is within a dominant prolongation). This reversal of roles in such internal formal areas is one of the most common features of traditional tonal music, and should be kept in mind as a possibility when you work out an analysis, the more so because bass-line sketches give priority to functional hierarchies. This dominant-prolonging tonic chord is an exception, but an important one.

In *Five Graphic Music Analyses*, the bass in the Bach chorale analysis, second middleground, shows two figures resulting from arpeggiation: 1) The coupling small a♭ to great A♭ in bars 1-5 is elaborated by a simple arpeggiation through the tonic chord (look at the score foreground to see how individual tones of this arpeggiation are prolonged); 2) The motion of the descending fifth (I-IV) in the final two measures is bisected into two thirds: a♭-f-d♭. The score foreground of Chopin, F-Major Etude, bars 1-8 (repetition in 15-22), has a simple leading-tone neighbor-note figure (=I-V$^6_5$-I).

[EXERCISES I.3; I.8, bars 1-10; I.20]

EXPANSION USING vi OR VI

In the first and second models of Ex. 1.13, vi (or VI) simply prolongs the tonic; in the remaining models, vi is the middle element in a foreground arpeggiation from I down to IV (or ii^6). The last model extends the series of thirds by including both scale degrees $\hat{4}$ and $\hat{2}$ (perhaps supporting IV and ii).

EXAMPLE 1.13 Expansion using vi or VI (tonic substitutes)

The first of Schubert's Wiener-Damen Walzer, D. 734, uses the major submediant (VI) to prolong I directly: I-VI-I-(ii)-V-I. See Ex. 1.14. The progression I-VI-I here articulates the formal and tonal design of a binary/ternary form. The thirteenth waltz from the same set (Ex. 1.15) corresponds to an expanded version of the last model of Ex. 1.13 (with Roman numerals I-vi-IV-ii), embellished primarily with secondary or applied dominants: V^7/vi in bar 7 is part of a i-V-i pattern tonicizing vi, and V^7/IV and V^7/ii in the B-section are embellishing chords. Also observe that formal design does not affect the bass notation in this instance: the E supporting vi is not an open note because it is only part of an expanded progression leading toward the dominant in bar 13, not a direct prolongation of the tonic, the function of the same note in the first waltz.

The notation for secondary or applied dominant and diminished chords is shown separately for reference in Ex. 1.16. As with other chromatic chords, these are treated as variants of diatonic chords with the same root and the bass is notated the same way (except for any added Roman numeral or figured-bass symbols, of course). When the progression involves a key region, secondary chords are usually notated as if in the new key. For additional illustrations, see Ex. 1.3 and the Introduction.

[EXERCISES I.9, I.23]

EXAMPLE 1.14 Schubert, Wiener-Damen Walzer, D. 734, no. 1

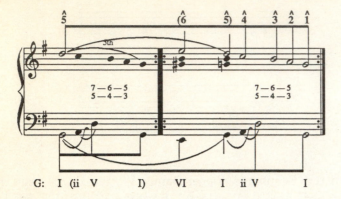

EXAMPLE 1.15 Schubert, Wiener-Damen Walzer, D. 734, no. 13

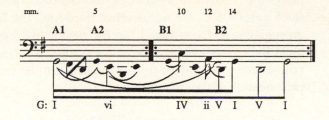

EXAMPLE 1.16 Secondary dominant and diminished chords

FILLING-IN OF HARMONIC INTERVALS IN FUNCTIONAL PATTERNS

A few common methods of filling in harmonic intervals appear in Ex. 1.17a: stepwise motion through the fifth from I to V , through the descending tonic-triad arpeggio, and through descending thirds. Many others are possible, such as lines with chromatic passing tones or with embellishments of some or all of the individual tones in the line. The first and second models in Ex. 1.17a involve the same notes but differ in their interpretations—you would choose one or the other depending on the situation. The first draws attention to the line filling the fifth but ignores any subdivisions according to functional groupings; the second shows those subdivisions but seems to break up the line. The first model is probably more appropriate for foreground events; the second may be used at any level.

EXAMPLE 1.17a Filling-in of harmonic intervals

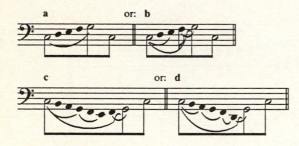

EXAMPLE 1.17b Alternate to the third model

An additional point about notation: In the third model, the third-line G-F-E is part of a descending tonic-chord arpeggiation, but the three notes E-F-G are not another third-line: the E belongs to the arpeggiation just mentioned, but F-G belong to the overall harmonic cycle. Ex. 1.17b shows an alternative reading for the same five notes, now understood as two third-lines because the entire pattern is a prolongation of the first dominant, G.

In Ex. 1.18, which expands Ex. 1.10, the arpeggiation I-V (G-D)—and the subordinate arpeggiation V: I-V (D-A) that follows—are filled in completely with steps, including chromatic passing tones which coincidentally form secondary or applied dominants. As in Ex. 1.3 earlier, the upper sketch is very detailed and follows all the chord changes in the score, and the lower sketch shows only the framework of the passage. Thinking only of the music in front of us, we might call the upper sketch a "foreground" bass and the lower sketch a "middleground" bass. In the context of the whole movement, more accurate labels would be the bass of "foreground 1" (lower) and "foreground 2" (upper).

In *Five Graphic Music Analyses*, the bass in the Bach chorale analysis, bars 6-11, fills in the space from V (e♭ in bar 6) to I (a♭ in bar 11) with a diatonic fourth-line (4-*Zug*) which also includes a chromatic passing tone, e♮. The score foreground of the C-Major Prelude shows the scalar filling-in of the coupling c'-c in bars 1-19; the steps of this line are accompanied in parallel tenths by the uppermost voice. In the Chopin C-Minor Etude, the motion I-V is filled in three times (see the second or third middleground); the second of these is a fully chromatic descent (see bars 21-41 of the score foreground) which expands the underlying diatonic descent of the middleground. A similar chromatic descent occurs in the score foreground of the F-Major Etude, bars 29-41.

[EXERCISES I.1; I.5; I.21]

EXAMPLE 1.18 Beethoven, Piano Sonata, op. 14, no. 2, I, bars 1-23

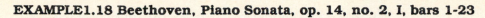

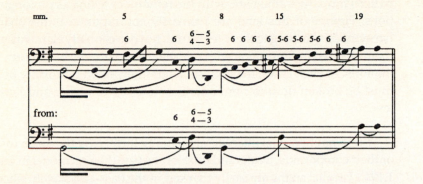

EXPANSION USING SEQUENTIAL PATTERNS, INCLUDING THE CIRCLE OF FIFTHS

The figures in Ex. 1.19 are often associated with traditional melodic sequences, but they also represent a more general class of repeated harmonic or voice-leading patterns or streams of parallel intervals, a class which Forte calls "linear intervallic patterns" (see his *Tonal Harmony in Concept and Practice*, Chapter 11; also, Forte and Gilbert, Chapter 4 (p. 83)). In order to interpret such patterns correctly, we must of course take into account more than the bass line, but we can still conveniently and accurately represent them in a bass-line sketch using traditional figured-bass symbols.

EXAMPLE 1.19a Expansion using sequential patterns

EXAMPLE 1.19b Interval patterns

Normally, the first and last chord (or two) of a linear intervallic pattern form the framework, with the remainder acting as prolongations. Figures of this kind are primarily contrapuntal rather than harmonic and belong to the foreground, but occasionally elements in them are used in connection with middleground or even background motions. In such cases, the pattern is not interpreted uniformly but must be broken up into components belonging to earlier and later levels.

Streams of parallel intervals are usually formed by thirds, sixths, or their compounds, tenths and thirteenths (see the first model in Ex. 1.19a). Parallel sixths are easily marked in the bass-line sketch, since they will typically form streams of parallel $\frac{6}{3}$ chords and thus can be identified with a series of figured-bass symbols "6." Parallel thirds or tenths may be treated similarly, using the figure "3" or "10."

The second and third models of Ex. 1.19a show forms of the diatonic "circle of fifths" progression, from which most other linear intervallic patterns derive. The voices to consider are the bass and the soprano (or main upper voice). Among the most common figures are the following: 5-6 or its reverse 6-5, 5-8 or its reverse 8-5, 5-10 or 10-5, 7-6 (but *not* 6-7), 7-10 or 10-7, and 8-10 or 10-8. Ex. 1.19b shows

examples of each of these with the second or third model as the bass.

Ex. 1.20 begins with a I-V-I foreground figure which is followed by a diatonic circle of fifths further embellished by filling thirds. The whole passage, then, follows the model of the first figure in Ex. 1.19a. Such patterns are especially common in Baroque music. Exs. 1.21 and 1.22, from Chopin Mazurkas, include readings of the main upper voice. In the first, the stream of parallel tenths is associated with a melodic sequence but the 5-10 series is not. In the second example, an extended 7-10 series is coupled with a chromatic circle of fifths pattern.

In *Five Graphic Music Analyses*, the score foreground of the C-Major Prelude shows a contrapuntal pattern of parallel tenths in bars 1-19. The insets above the score foreground of the Bach chorale analysis show the origin of the progression of bars 8-10 in a similar pattern of parallel tenths.

[EXERCISE I.8]

EXAMPLE 1.22 Chopin, Mazurka, op. 67, no. 2, bars 21-24

EXAMPLE 1.20 J. S. Bach, Invention in G Major, bars 1-7

EXAMPLE 1.21 Chopin, Mazurka, op. 6, no. 1, bars 1-10

IMPLIED NOTES

Notes in parentheses in the bass-line sketch are "implied"; that is, the requirements of the earlier structural levels lead us to expect some tone to occur in a particular place, but due to rhythmic displacement or some interfering voice-leading event, the tone does not actually sound or else sounds in the wrong octave. Implied notes are generally more appropriate to the upper parts, but two instances proper to the bass are shown in Ex. 1.23. The first model shows the unusual case of a first-inversion structural dominant, which may occur at either

middleground or background—by the notation here, the latter is assumed. In this instance, it is acceptable to notate the implied root of the dominant. The second model shows a somewhat more common phenomenon: the opening tonic harmony lacks its root in the bass. The clarity of the bass-line sketch is assured by showing this implied structural tonic tone. This model is also useful for those nineteenth-century pieces which do not begin with tonic harmony (though they may define the tonic key in other ways) but move clearly to the dominant or other degree at the first main structural division.

EXAMPLE 1.23 Implied notes

The opening of Debussy's Prelude to "The Afternoon of a Faun" is sketched in Ex. 1.24. The implied tones in the first three bars supply the correct bass for the solo flute melody which is all that is directly heard in these bars. Great A♯ and B are prefixes to E, read here as the first note of the stuctural bass arpeggiation E-F♯-B-E, or I-ii-V-I, which governs the harmony in the entire Prelude. (A bass-line sketch for the whole composition is discussed in Chapter 2 below.)

EXAMPLE 1.24 Debussy, Prelude to "The Afternoon of a Faun," bars 1-13

Schenker uses notes in parentheses for two or three different purposes. Two instances in *Five Graphic Music Analyses* where implied notes are used in the manner described above are: 1) Haydn E♭-Sonata, second foreground (middle system), beginning. Here the chord in the treble staff shows pitches which we assume to be the correct disposition of the upper voices from the exposition (whose main features are given in capsule form at the upper left corner). The two notes in parentheses at that point in the score foreground have the same source. 2) Chopin F-Major Etude, third middleground and score foreground, bar 55, bass. The bass arpeggiation leads us to expect great C, but the score has only c'. In the Bach chorale analysis, bars 3 and 9, Schenker uses parentheses for a different purpose: as a way to isolate decorative tones which are not part of the main foreground progression.

THE SUBDOMINANT

The first model in Ex. 1.25 shows a background dividing subdominant, a rare occurrence even in the later nineteenth-century music where you might encounter it. The other models show more typical cases. In the second, the two subdominants function quite differently: a divider first embellishes I (as I-IV-I) but another subdominant then leads to V. The third model shows an alternate notation which you may use if the subdominant divider seems more important or you wish to bring it out in the graph. The fifth and sixth models show variants of models in Ex. 1.9 above. In the first case, the descending sixth, small c to E, is prolonged by a subdominant arpeggiation, with the F as neighbor note resolving to E supporting I^6. In the second case, the E itself is a neighbor note prolonging F. Which notation you should use obviously depends on the circumstances of the particular piece.

EXAMPLE 1.25 The subdominant

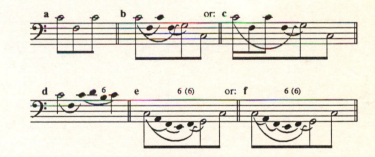

The second model is realized in Ex. 1.26, from the Chopin Mazurka, op. 33, no. 1. Embellishing (foreground) subdominant arpeggiations prolong the tonic within the framework of two simple i-V-i motions. Similarly, in Ex.1.27, the subdominant is merely a surface embellishment of the tonic in the second part of a simple binary form, not part of a functional cycle (note that the tonic of bar 14 moves directly to the structural dominant of bar 15).

[EXERCISES I.18, I.26]

23

EXAMPLE 1.26 Chopin, Mazurka, op. 33, no. 1, bars 1-12　　　**EXAMPLE 1.27 Schubert, Deutscher Tanz, D.970, no. 4**

THE "DECEPTIVE CADENCE"

The deceptive cadence to vi (or VI in the minor key) and similar progressions are normally treated as a prolongation of the dominant, as in the first model of Ex. 1.28, but in some instances it is better understood as prolonging the tonic, through I-vi. The decision, as usual, depends on context. In general, take the second choice only if the vi is a middleground harmony or key region. Otherwise, take the first. (The underlying idea of the expansion of the V is that tension in the dominant is not resolved by the deceptive move to vi, but actually heightened; it is only when the true tonic arrives that the tension is removed.)

Ex.1.29 interprets the exposition, closing theme, in the Beethoven Sonata whose opening bars we have inspected earlier (Exs. 1.10, 1.18). Through expansion by simple and varied repetition, vi helps to prolong (and dramatically amplify) a middleground dominant chord established in bar 51. Note that the interlocking slurs are missing for the ii returning to V in bars 53 and 57. In both cases, these predominants are foreground elaborations *within* the dominant prolongation and thus are not actually part of the middleground functional progression (here, I-V-I in bars 26, 51 and 58, respectively).

EXAMPLE 1.28 The deceptive cadence

EXAMPLE 1.29 Beethoven, Piano Sonata, op. 14, no. 2, I, bars 47-63

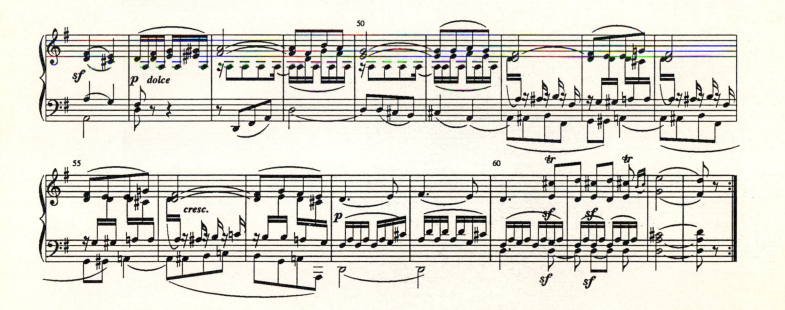

In Ex. 1.30, the VI in bar 12 belongs to the foreground but, nevertheless, is better understood as a tonic extension, rather than as a dominant prolongation. Form-design factors play a role: the strict four-bar phrase design and the parallelism with the first phrase: bars 1–4 have i–V⁷–i; bars 9–12 i–V⁷–VI (as clear functional substitute for i). As a result, it is very difficult to hear bars 12–14 as a single unit expanding the dominant.

In *Five Graphic Music Analyses*, the Haydn Sonata analysis includes an extended prolongation of vi within the V that is the underlying harmony of the entire development (see the bass of the top system for the V; see bars 81–111 of the other levels for the vi, which changes to VI (as V/ii) near the end of the passage).

[EXERCISE I.7]

EXAMPLE 1.30 Chopin, Mazurka, op. 7, no. 2, section A

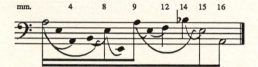

THE MINOR KEY

Most bass progressions are common to both major and minor keys, but the latter does have some traits peculiar to it. Prominent among these are the dominant-minor key region and the related alteration of v to V (that is, V♭–♮) or its reverse (V♮–♭), but these do not generally affect the interpretation of the bass. Another is the tendency toward enhanced chromaticism, especially in descending lines, as in several of the models in Ex. 1.31. In Ex. 1.32, the famous chaconne bass of the Baroque era (stepwise descent from the tonic to the dominant in the bass) appears here in a completely chromatic form and accomplishes a repeated linear expansion of the initial i-V in a i-V-i bass

EXAMPLE 1.31 Common bass progressions in minor keys

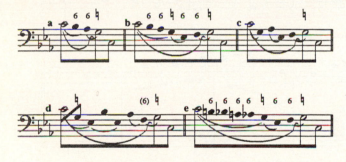

arpeggiation. (See the similar progressions in the Chopin C-Minor Etude analysis in *Five Graphic Music Analyses*.)

Still another minor-key trait is often crucial to readings of the bass line: the prominence of III (and its key region) gives rise to arpeggiations with almost any combination of motions between i, III, and V (or v), including i-III-i, i-V-III, or i-v-III-i, among others. It is very often appropriate to show such patterns with open notes, if they belong to the background or early middleground. In general, be prepared to assign to III greater structural importance in the minor key than in the major. The score for the first section of the Chopin Mazurka, op. 67, no. 2 is reproduced in Ex. 1.33, but the bass-line sketch includes a background reading for the entire piece. A straightforward i-III-V arpeggiation prolongs i twice in the A-section. This pattern, as it happens, maps onto the tonal structure of the entire piece:

	A	Trio	transition	A reprise
G minor:	i	III	V	i

EXAMPLE 1.32 C. P. E. Bach, Sonatas, Rondos, and Fantasies, Vol. 1, Sonata no. 3, II, rondo theme

EXAMPLE 1.33 Chopin, Mazurka in G Minor, op. 67, no. 2 (first section only)

UNFOLDING: A SPECIAL SYMBOL

It will be a good exercise for you to examine this bass-line sketch closely. The tonic-triad arpeggiation expands i in bars 2-6. What happens in bars 6-8, and what background or middleground element do the events prolong? What is the governing middleground progression in bars 1-10? What precisely does the slur from small c in bar 8 to small d in bar 9 mean?

[EXERCISE I.27]

Unfolding is the linear presentation of an underlying harmonic interval. Thirds and sixths are the intervals most often unfolded; the first model in Ex. 1.34 shows this—the melodic succession small b-g unfolds a third that is an interval of the dominant harmony. The same figure might have been notated with a simple slur, but the unfolding symbol gives special attention to the interval spanned. (Unfolded thirds are used in Exs. 1.10, 1.15, and 1.18 above.) Unfolding is especially useful to bring out voice-leading patterns when several intervals are unfolded in a row, as often happens (see, for instance, Exs. 2.3-2.6).

EXAMPLE 1.34 Unfolding in the bass

Motions which may be best interpreted using unfolding are more likely to occur in the upper parts than in the bass, if only because unfolding is a feature of the foreground and the kind of elaboration that gives rise to it is more likely in the upper parts. In the bass, the unfolding symbol has a few additional, specialized uses:

1. When linear motion in a cadence is to be emphasized over root motion (functional pattern), as in the second model of Ex. 1.34, where emphasis is on the third-line small e-d-c, rather than the functional progression V-I;

2. When a direct melodic motion of the tritone occurs, as in the third model (direct resolution of the first or upper tone—here, c′—is not required); and

3. When a I-V succession occurs in a half-cadence, but the succeeding phrase does not close the functional cycle, as in the last model (which assumes a continuation other than i or V).

A point of notational detail: Always write the unfolding symbol so that the stems of the notes point "inward," that is, toward the center of the interval being unfolded. This makes a much more compact, better-looking symbol than pointing the stems "outward" or away from the interval.

Ex. 1.35, from a short character piece by Schumann, follows the third model, using the tritone small g-c♯ to expand a foreground bass arpeggiation I-V-I in bars 1-3. The progression is repeated exactly in bars 3-5. This example has the added feature of resolutions of both tritone notes in another unfolding, the third small d-f♯.

EXAMPLE 1.35 Schumann, "Von fremden Ländern und Menschen," op. 15, no. 1, bars 1-8

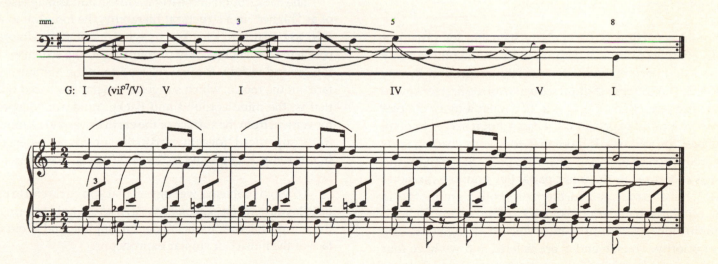

In *Five Graphic Music Analyses*, the score foreground for the Haydn Sonata analysis, bars 112-116, shows paired thirds (actually compound tenths!) as unfoldings. An isolated diminshed fifth appears in bars 122-123. The unfolded fourth in the bass system, second middleground and later levels for Chopin, F-Major Etude, bars 51-55, follows model one above. Most of the unfoldings in the bass of the score foreground simply point out octave duplications.

[EXERCISES I.2, I.17, I.24]

CHORDAL REDUCTION

In analytic work, it is sometimes helpful to bridge the gap between the score and an interpreted foreground with a chordal reduction, a relatively informal reading that separates embellishing notes from the basic voice leading. A chordal reduction is essentially the text of the score (including bar-lines) with non-harmonic notes removed, plain voice leading identified insofar as possible (to accomplish this, octave positions of some notes may have to be corrected), a few devices appropriate to the foreground identified (if desired), and the harmonic basis identified. (The "rhythmic reduction" of Forte and Gilbert, p. 136, is the same as our chordal reduction.) In some circumstances, it might even be appropriate to use such a graph as the score foreground for a set of analysis graphs.

The chordal reduction is particularly valuable for ornate or harmonically complex compositions but can also be helpful as a way to doublecheck the interpretation of details of the foreground. By way of illustration, Ex. 1.36 offers a chordal reduction of the first seventeen bars of Schumann, op. 68, no. 14. This is, of course, a much simpler problem than you could expect in most cases, but it serves to demonstrate the basic procedures. If more than four voice-leading parts are present, reduction to four-part texture is preferred; remove duplicated tones or figures in the inner parts. For example, six notes sound in bar 1, but d' is repeated; furthermore, both d's move to e' in the next bar. Similarly, b in the left hand of bar 1 moves to c' in bar 2, but this motion duplicates the upper-most voice (b'-c''), which clearly should have priority. Thus, b and c' are deleted and we have four voices in each chord in bars 1 and 2. Examine the rest of Ex. 1.36 to see

if you can justify the note choices.

The score foreground for the C-Major Prelude in *Five Graphic Music Analyses* is a simple chordal reduction of that composition's arpeggiations.

[EXERCISE I.6]

METAPHORS FOR THE STRUCTURAL LEVELS

There is some confusion in the literature due to description of the structural levels using adjectives that reflect conflicting metaphors and also opposing emphases (composing-out versus reduction). You should be aware of this problem for your own reading as well as in writing commentaries on graphs.

In *Five Graphic Music Analyses*, Schenker places the background at the beginning of each set of graphs and at the top of the page. Thus, as the reader follows downward from the background to foreground, he or she traces the path of composing-out and may refer naturally to the background and first or second middlegrounds as "early," the other middlegrounds and foreground as "later." This is the manner of description and presentation we prefer.

The background and early middlegrounds may also be thought of as "higher" in a structural hierarchy, the foreground as "lower"; this, too, matches Schenker's page presentation. Unfortunately, it conflicts with another way of referring to the structural levels. The foreground vicinity is often referred to in the literature as the "surface" of the music, which suggests a metaphor based on reduction; that is, the middleground and background are "deeper" (as if in movement from the surface of the earth inward to its foundations, or from "superficial" ideas inward to the "profound" essence of a thing). In this sense, background is "lower" (that is, deeper).

To avoid problems, we suggest that you be careful to use the same page layout as in *Five Graphic Music Analyses*, hold to terms that reflect the composing-out "earlier/later" metaphor, and avoid using "surface of the music" or similar expressions.

EXAMPLE 1.36 Schumann, "A Short Study," op. 68, no. 14, bars 1-17, chordal reduction

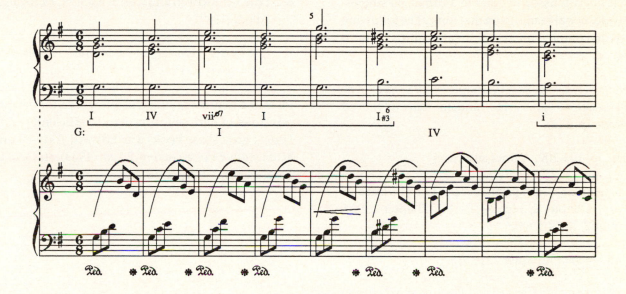

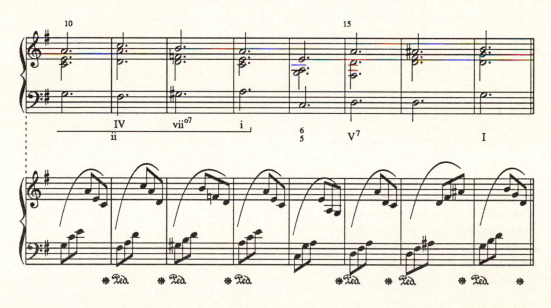

FURTHER READING

The bass-line sketch is not discussed in other texts; thus, no suggestions can be made for additional readings on that topic. The following are presentations of harmonic functional relationships from a Schenkerian perspective.

1. Felix Salzer, *Structural Hearing*, Part II, Chapter 4 (p. 87); also, the opening pages of Chapter 5 (pp. 97-118); and, for more advanced problems, Chapter 6 (p. 148).

2. Forte and Gilbert, pp. 103-109. A brief summary.

3. Schenker, *Free Composition*, see in particular pp. 111-117, but also the following: Part I, Chapter 2, 3 (p. 14); Part II, Chapter 2, 1 (p. 29); Part III, Chapter 2, B, 1 (p. 68).[2]

4. Oswald Jonas, *Introduction*, Chapter 2 (p. 37).

5. Allen Forte, *Tonal Harmony in Concept and Practice*, third edition (1979). This is a standard harmony textbook whose exposition of the subject is closely tied to a Schenkerian viewpoint but concentrates on the harmonic aspect and avoids the graphic notation. The book could serve as extended review or background reading.

6. Edward Aldwell and Carl Schachter, *Harmony and Voice-Leading*, 2d ed. (1989).

7. Joel Lester, *Harmony in Tonal Music*, 2 vols. (1982).

Two other current harmony textbooks are based on Schenkerian ideas and may serve as useful references, though neither presents the principles of harmonic functions so efficiently and concisely as does Forte's text. These books are: Edward Aldwell and Carl Schachter, *Harmony and Voice-Leading*, 2d ed. (1989); and Joel Lester, *Harmony in Tonal Music*, 2 vols. (1982).

---

[2]Schenker's *Harmony* is the first volume in the trilogy that concluded with *Free Composition* (the middle volume is the two-part *Counterpoint*). The *Harmony* is a fascinating period document with some excellent insights into harmonic practice, but it was published in 1906, long before the development of the analytic method beginning in the *Tonwille* journal series (1921-24). Its use as a reference source, thus, is limited.

Chapter 2: Four Analysis Narratives

The steps needed to construct a bass analysis are the following:

1. Listen to or play the composition and decide on its formal design.
2. Align the open-note I-V-I groups within that design.
3. Locate subordinate I-V-I groups associated with smaller form units, such as phrases or periods, depending on the length of the piece, and doublecheck the notation to be sure the hierarchies are correctly represented.
4. Interpret the remaining bass motions, which will lead to and from the several tonic and dominant tones already identified.

The first of the four narratives below discusses the application of each of these steps in some detail. The other narratives are more in the nature of comments on special stylistic features that might pose obstacles to working out an analysis.

BEETHOVEN, SYMPHONY NO. 2, III, SCHERZO

Listen to the movement several times and play through the keyboard reduction given in Ex. 2.1. (We are not including the Trio.)

The first task in analysis is to determine the formal design of the composition, in order to aid placement of the open notes in the structural bass arpeggiations. Since we expect a scherzo to be written in one of the eighteenth-century dance forms, we can consult the descriptions in Chapter 3 below. The rounded binary form fits best, and the two I-V-I patterns can be aligned with it as in Ex. 2.2. The first V is placed in bar 13, at the point the dominant key region is clearly defined and its tonic plainly presented for the first time. (The alternative, if V were not clearly defined or if the rhythmic or dramatic momentum drives beyond, would be to choose the final V in the section.) The second I is very clear; it coincides with the beginning of the reprise, as we would expect. The last V-I is problematic because of the frequent repetition of cadential patterns in the final 20 bars. bars 81-83 were chosen because of the finality of the gesture: the previous cadences have 3̂ above, and the final V-I has the effect of an emphatic

reiteration, the "afterbeat" effect that is a central rhythmic and motivic feature of this movement.

EXAMPLE 2.2 Beethoven, Symphony No. 2, III, Scherzo, bass sketch

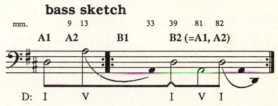

Within A, the first task is to identify any additional I-V-I patterns associated with the two eight-bar phrases. Other than this, the main problem is deciding how to treat the surface third-lines, such as the D-E-F♯ in bar 1. These may be presented as linear intervals of the third (without the passing tone), with the notes slurred; as lines of the third, with the notes slurred; or as unfolded thirds, with or without the passing tone (the options are shown in Ex. 2.3). As Ex. 2.4 shows, we chose the unfolded third to emphasize the separation between the lower note (which belongs to the bass line) and the upper (which is an embellishing inner voice). The passing tone was retained because the sketch is meant to be complete.

EXAMPLE 2.3 Beethoven, Symphony No. 2, III, bars 1-4, options for bass sketch

EXAMPLE 2.4 Beethoven, Symphony No. 2, III, bars 1-16, bass sketch

33

In section B, we assume that V (the open note from bar 13) is prolonged throughout. First, locate the expected recurrence of V at the end of the section. Then, if it is clear, trace the immediate approach to the V. In this case, half steps move about great A (B♭-A-G♯). [begin footnote] Note that the D-minor second-inversion chord in bar 30 is merely a passing chord—generated by the passing tone A in the bass—not part of a cadential dominant figure. [end footnote] Finally, identify the remaining patterns of motion. Here, it is simply a pair of fourths, A-D, F♯-B♭, filled in by the main motive. See Ex. 2.5.

EXAMPLE 2.1 Beethoven, Symphony No. 2, piano reduction

EXAMPLE 2.1 continued

EXAMPLE 2.5 Beethoven, Symphony No. 2, III, bars 17-39, bass sketch

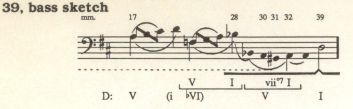

In the reprise, the main task is to identify and assess any deviations from the opening. Here, the first ten bars are identical to the opening. Then, an extension which moves above the bass shifts the mode (♮-♭) before paired fifths appear (C♮-F♮, A-D) in a pattern very similar to the opening of section B, the control middleground figure being a triad arpeggiation, D-F♮-A-D. This material is simply repeated until the final cadence. See Ex. 2.6.

EXAMPLE 2.6 Beethoven, Symphony No. 2, III, bars 39-84, bass sketch

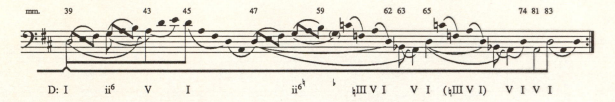

BRAHMS, INTERMEZZO IN A MINOR, OP. 76, NO. 7

Emphasis on all three degrees of the tonic triad—as $\hat{1}$, $\hat{3}$, $\hat{5}$, or i, III, and V (or v)—is a special feature of the minor key and often acts as a combined melodic/harmonic motive. In this Intermezzo, this motive acts at a number of levels, from the surface to the tonal design of the whole, to develop a tightly knit, organic design very characteristic of Brahms. (One could argue that Schenker's analytic method is more appropriate to the music of Brahms than to any other.)

Formal design poses an initial problem, for the composer has placed a compact rounded binary form (mediant cadence) within the frame of an apparently unrelated eight-bar passage stated at the beginning and repeated literally at the end. Such a design can pose serious difficulties for analysis of the upper voices (where does the first tone of the fundamental line lie?), but usually does not affect the bass analysis. If the tonic sonority is clearly presented in the introduction (as it is here), then it is given an open note. If the tonic is not clearly stated until the first main section, then the introduction is considered to be a foreground prefix.

The introduction is tonally closed. Section A (bar 9) begins with i6 and ends on the mediant; section B1 moves toward the dominant (in bar 24), and the altered reprise begins again with i6 in bar 25, concluding with a strongly defined, drawn-out cadence with tonic-pedal extension in bars 28-34. A brief transition moves to the dominant before the introduction is given again as the coda.

The bass motions that correspond with this description are shown in Ex. 2.7. A detailed reading of the harmony appears in Ex. 2.8, which includes some notations relating to the motivic arpeggiations. The score appears in Example 2.9.

EXAMPLE 2.7 Brahms, Intermezzo, op. 76, No. 7, bass sketch (background)

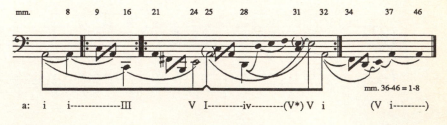

*I6; should be cadential dominant

EXAMPLE 2.9 Brahms, Intermezzo, op. 76, No. 7

EXAMPLE 2.9 continued

EXAMPLE 2.8 Brahms, Intermezzo, op. 76, No. 7, bass sketch (foreground)

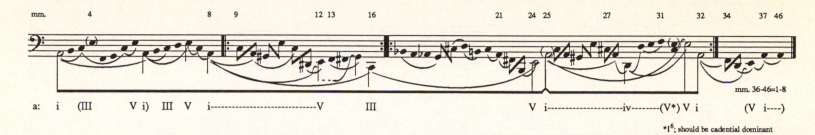

mm. 36-46=1-8

*I⁶; should be cadential dominant

DEBUSSY, PRELUDE TO "THE AFTERNOON OF A FAUN," OPENING

A bass-line sketch can be very useful even in compositions where it is not always possible to read harmonic functions consistently throughout. Debussy's famous orchestral prelude may serve as representative of a substantial repertory in the late nineteenth and early twentieth centuries in which the large-scale tonal framework still operates but in which many details of the surface are functionally ambiguous. It also serves to demonstrate the value of the bass-line sketch for obtaining an analytic understanding of tonal and harmonic motions in extended nineteenth-century compositions (where it is sometimes almost impossible to reach an unequivocal reading of the upper parts).

Two sketches are given below: Ex. 2.10 is a background/middleground sketch of the entire composition. An extended bass arpeggiation I-V-I is followed by a chromatic mediant (I-VI-I) and final structural bass arpeggiation. Ex. 2.11 shows the details of the first structural motion, I-V, covering bars 1-30. Note in particular the opening bars. Despite the functional attenuation achieved by the B♭⁷ chord and the functional uncertainty of the D-major⁷ chord, it is not difficult to place both within a functionally stable context and to explain their presence, if not harmonically, then motivically: the B♭ derives from the A♯-B chromatic neighbor; the D♮ is the first tone of another chromatic neighbor pair, D♮-D♯).

Felix Salzer includes a complete graph of the opening section (bars 1-30) in *Structural Hearing*, Fig. 455. The text discussion, which concentrates on the opening flute melody and its consequences, is in vol. 1, pp. 209-210. As an example of extended treatment of issues in music at the turn of the century, see Christopher O. Lewis, *Tonal Coherence in Mahler's Ninth Symphony* (Ann Arbor 1984). Lewis uses Schenkerian methods, but often relies heavily on the bass and is obliged to make notational adjustments to accommodate the technique of "double tonics."

EXAMPLE 2.10 Debussy, Prelude to "The Afternoon of a Faun," bass sketch (background/middleground)

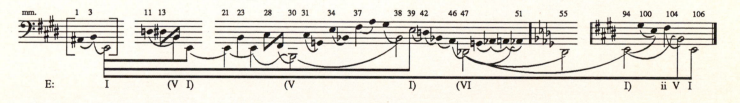

EXAMPLE 2.11 Debussy, Prelude to "The Afternoon of a Faun," bars 1-30 bass sketch (foreground)

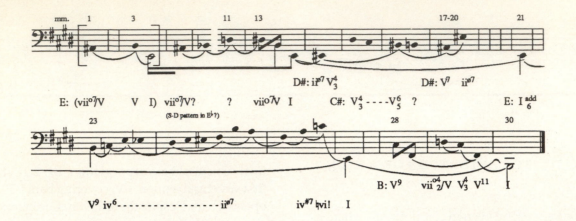

DEBUSSY, PRELUDE "THE ENGULFED CATHEDRAL"

This is essentially a footnote to the preceding section—an extreme case, a composition in which the harmonic surface is very complex, in which simply determining the <u>exact</u> components of a chord is often a difficult, even hopeless, task, but in which—one might say, ironically—the underlying motions of the bass are few, direct, and very comprehensible. Ex. 2.12 shows these motions. Note that, as in the Prelude to "The Afternoon of a Faun," these motions are a combination of I-V-I and mediant figures. The point of all this is that the power of the bass to organize is very great and probably applies even to a wider range of music than the traditional major-minor repertoire. (A passage from this Prelude is examined in greater detail in Chapter 9 below.)

EXAMPLE 2.12 Debussy, Prelude "The Engulfed Cathedral," bass sketch (background)

Chapter 3: Structural Bass Patterns and Formal Design

Formal design is one of the principal means of determining the hierarchies of structural levels for a bass-line sketch. In this chapter, we list the most common formal patterns associated with instrumental dance forms (and related or derivative music) from the seventeenth to mid-nineteenth centuries.

This repertoire includes the many dances brought into French ballet and opera by Lully, the stylized older dances and other movements in the Italian instrumental music of Corelli and others, dance movements in the later Baroque (as in the keyboard suites of Bach and Handel), the menuets of the Classical period (and often slow movements of sonatas or quartets, also), and the small character pieces, waltzes, galops, and mazurkas of Schubert, Chopin, Schumann, and others. In the later eighteenth century in particular, many songs also were written in these forms, or variants of them. Even larger vocal solo pieces, such as operatic operas, very often relied on rather complex, expanded versions of these forms.

We should emphasize that the categories below cover stereotypical patterning; thus, they can account for the great majority of compositions, but cannot be expected to account for every possible piece. Furthermore, we are dealing only with gross features of formal design; there would be little value for our purposes here in trying to bring down the categories to the level of the patterning of phrases and periods, since the resulting list would be very long and too difficult to use efficiently (assuming it could be constructed at all).

The Preface above gives our reasons for not using Schenker's own form labels. Unfortunately, there is no consistency in other currently available textbooks with respect to the terminology used for the study of form types. The labels we have adopted here are, in part at least, refinements of those found in Peter Spencer and Peter M. Temko, *A Practical Approach to the Study of Form in Music*. Variants occurring in certain other books are given in notes under each heading.

SIMPLE BINARY FORM (TONIC)

We have divided the class of simple binary forms into two types, depending on the harmony which closes the first half, or A-section. The simple binary form is perhaps the most common of all forms in the later seventeenth and eighteenth centuries. In instrumental music, this design will usually have the familiar pairs of repeat signs conveniently articulating two sections, "A" and "B."

The word "simple" refers to the lack of a thematic reprise (or at least a clear reprise) at the point that the structural tonic tone returns in the B-section. The sub-category "tonic" indicates that the A-section closes on tonic harmony (this is shown in Ex. 3.1 below with a closed note). This type is less common than its counterpart among the forms with thematic reprise, the binary/ternary. As one instance of a simple binary form (tonic), see Example 1.27 (Schubert, Deutscher Tanz, D. 970, no. 4).

Two other characteristics of all the simple binary forms may also be mentioned: the two sections normally have very limited thematic/motivic differentiation; and section B is usually longer than section A. In the B-section, B1 may reach the dominant as the goal of its overall harmonic process, which is what the placement of notes in Ex. 3.1 suggests, or the dominant may be stated immediately and prolonged. Both processes are very commonly found. Also, the beginning of B2 may be coincident with the clear re-establishment of the tonic, or the tonic may just be "hinted at," to be reached conclusively only near or in the final cadence.

The placement of labels and notes in Example 3.1 should be regarded only as indications of general positions on the time line of the piece. The labels A1, A2, B1, B2, refer to the common articulation of each main section in small binary dances into two equal or roughly equal parts (such as two eight-bar phrases or phrase pairs). Three-phrase sections do occur, but infrequently (labels A1, A2, A3 or B1, B2, B3). Larger binary forms often are not articulated so plainly.

EXAMPLE 3.1 Simple binary form, tonic type

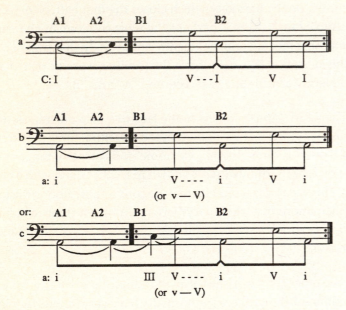

Note on the problem of thematic reprise: One can, of course, argue over what constitutes a clear reprise, especially in some of the more motivically dense dance movements in Bach suites. We intend "simple binary" as a kind of default to subsume such cases, as opposed to the binary/ternary design, which has an extensive, usually literal reprise, and is the most commonly found formal design in Classical-period menuets.

Note on terminology: Spencer and Temko use "simple binary form" in a slightly different way than we do here: for them, the term refers to what we call "simple binary (non-tonic)" below; that is, where the goal harmony at the end of A is some chord other than the tonic. Otherwise, the characteristics of the design are the same. They never mention an equivalent of our "tonic" type. Wallace Berry, in *Form in Music*, uses "incipient binary" for cases which would seem to include our "simple binary (tonic)." Robert Gauldin, in *A Practical Approach to Eighteenth-Century Counterpoint*, supplies a section heading "simple two-reprise form," "two-reprise" being a frequently used synonym for "binary." He contrasts "simple" with "extended," which suggests that length is the primary distinction, though he discusses a set of typical characteristics for each type, such as the motivic consistency of the simple two-reprise forms or possible reprise and more complex tonal motion of the extended forms. Douglass Green's term "sectional simple binary" form seems to be identical to our "simple binary (tonic)." His terms are also used by Stefan Kostka and Dorothy Payne in their *Tonal Harmony*.

Finally, the formal design stereotype we call binary form here is *not* synonymous with what Schenker calls "two-part form," even though it might seem to be to a reader of Forte and Gilbert's presentation (Chapter 16, p. 208) (see the comments at the end of this chapter). Schenker distinguished between "inner" and "outer form": for him traditional formal designs are the surface result of underlying tonal events, and thus he divided (inner) forms into one to five-part designs depending on the tonal features of the first middleground. "Two-part" inner form may, thus, be the basis of a variety of "outer" forms which may or may not have two sections. See *Free Composition*, Part III, Chapter 5, for Schenker's own presentation of his form theory. A particularly clear presentation of the notion of "inner" and "outer form" is given by Salzer in *Structural Hearing*, Chapter 8, pp. 223 ff.

SIMPLE BINARY FORM (NON-TONIC)

The simple binary (non-tonic) design has most of the same general characteristics as the tonic type, including the two main sections, "A" and "B," with subdivisions A1, A2, B1, and B2, motion toward the dominant or prolongation of the dominant, and lack of a clear thematic reprise at B2. Of the possible non-tonic degrees for the cadence of the A-section, the dominant (in major or minor keys) and mediant (most often in minor, occasionally in major) are by far the most common (see the models in Exs. 3.2 and 3.3). Motion to the submediant (in major or minor) is somewhat less likely; other degrees are rare.

Of the several simple binary forms, the dominant type is certainly the most frequently found in the seventeenth and eighteenth centuries; in fact, it may be the most common of all forms in that era. Division B1 in this type must prolong the dominant. A brief return to the tonic is common at its beginning, but this should be interpreted as foreground elaboration of the structural dominant, not as a structural return. See Ex. 3.4, the well-known Gavotte from Bach's G-Major French Suite. Note the temporary tonic in bar 10, the more extensive tonicization of vi (E Minor) in bars 11-16 (also part of the dominant prolongation), and the difficulty in establishing a point for the structural tonic note anywhere before the final cadence, even though we can tell that we are in the tonic key for at least the last seven bars. All these traits are quite typical of pieces using the simple binary (dominant) design.

The simple binary (mediant) in the minor key is also very common in the eighteenth century, but the major-key form and the less likely submediant types belong to the nineteenth century. See Example 1.15: Schubert, Waltz, D. 734, no. 13 (mediant, major key).

Note on terminology: Simple binary (non-tonic) corresponds to what Spencer and Temko call "simple binary form," to Douglass Green's "continuous simple binary," and apparently to Wallace Berry's category "full binary," except perhaps for the smallest (sixteen-bar) dances.

EXAMPLE 3.2   Simple binary form (dominant)

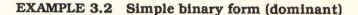
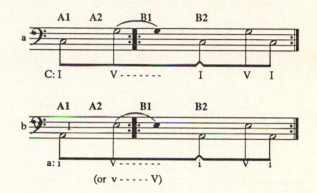

EXAMPLE 3.3 Simple binary form (mediant)

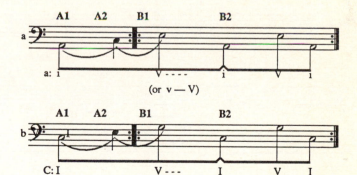

43

EXAMPLE 3.4 J. S. Bach, French Suite in G Major, Gavotte

TERNARY ("SIMPLE RONDO")

Before labelling any form design "ternary," be sure to look at the two sections below ("Binary/ternary" and "Rounded binary"), which describe three-part forms within the two-part binary frame. As it is given here, the ternary design is often more useful for solo vocal music (as in some rondos in Mozart's comic operas) than it is for instrumental dances, but one may occasionally find small baroque rondeaux with only one couplet or digression. Still, with extensions, this design can serve for the many Baroque rondeaux and later five-part or seven-part Classical rondos. The largest of the Baroque vocal forms, the da capo aria, may also be referred here.

See the model for the ternary form in Ex. 3.5, then examine Ex. 3.6, Purcell, Choice Collection of Lessons..., Rondo. (The score for this appears in the exercises for Part II.) There are two couplets, and we

EXAMPLE 3.5 Ternary form ("simple rondo")

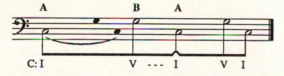

**EXAMPLE 3.6 Purcell, Choice Collection of Lessons...,
Rondo from *Abdelazer***

might therefore predict three structural I-V-I groups, but because the first couplet is in the relative major, there are actually only two such groups. Also see Ex. 3.7. Couperin, *Les baricades mistérieuses*. Here, with three couplets, we have the expected four structural I-V-I groups. Notice that in each couplet, tonal motion is toward a dominant that appears at or near the end.

EXAMPLE 3.7 Couperin, *Les baricades mistérieuses*

Note on terminology: Spencer and Temko use "simple ternary form" in the same way we use "ternary" here. Wallace Berry also uses "simple ternary form" but it includes our binary/ternary and rounded binary as well as our ternary design. For him, "incipient ternary" is distinguished only by the briefness of its reprise (a problematic criterion). Our term would appear to correspond to Douglass Green's "sectional ternary" form, though his discussion of the term is not entirely clear. Finally, ternary form as it is identified here is *not* synonymous with what Schenker calls "three-part form."

[EXERCISE I.6]

BINARY/TERNARY

The binary/ternary form is a hybrid of the simple binary (tonic) and the ternary form: a three-part form within the two-part binary frame. In both major and minor keys, the bass-line sketch will be the same as for simple binary (tonic), with the restriction that the return of the tonic and the beginning of B2 (that is, the thematic reprise) must coincide (Ex. 3.8). The reprise in B2 is usually literal and may consist of A1 only (with appropriate cadence) or A1 and A2 both. The latter is the norm in Classical menuets and their trios, where the binary/ternary design appears more often than any other type.

EXAMPLE 3.8 Binary/ternary

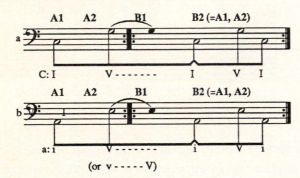

Be sure not to confuse the binary/ternary form with "composite ternary," a term used by most writers to refer to the overall design of a menuet-trio movement: a menuet is likely to be in binary/ternary form, its trio likewise; the combination of menuet-trio-menuet reprise is a composite ternary form.

There are several representatives of binary/ternary form among the musical examples in this book: see, for instance, Exs. 1.3 (Schubert, D. 779, no. 3) and 1.11 (Mozart, Symphony No. 35, III, Trio).

Note on terminology: Spencer and Temko never mention directly a design of the type described here. Berry's "simple ternary" includes both binary/ternary and rounded binary design. Kostka and Payne call the design "two-reprise continuous ternary form," though Green refers to it as "sectional rounded binary."

[EXERCISES I.22, I.25]

ROUNDED BINARY

Like the binary/ternary form, the rounded binary design is a three-part form within the two-part binary frame, this time mixing the simple binary (dominant)—or, occasionally, one of the other non-tonic types—with the ternary form. In both major and minor keys, the bass-line sketch will be the same as for the simple binary (dominant), but the return of tonic and the thematic reprise (at B2) must coincide (Ex. 3.9).

Unlike the binary/ternary design, the rounded binary design suffers a wider range of literalness and completeness in its reprise: it may consist of A1 only (with appropriate cadence), A1 and A2 both, or a clearly defined opening segment of A1 followed by variation or development of the original material. The latter is apt to occur in the most stylized examples of Baroque dances which normally are simpler in design, such as the gavotte or bourrée. A reprise of A2 only—without A1—is often called "balanced binary" and is best known through the sonatas of Scarlatti, though it is occasionally found in Baroque dance movements as well. In such cases, the structural tonic may return at some point after the beginning of B2, not coincident with it.

See Exs. 1.12 (Haydn, Sonata in C, Menuet) and 2.1-2.6 (Beethoven, Symphony No. 2, III, Scherzo) for instances of the rounded binary design.

Note on terminology: Spencer and Temko use "rounded binary" as we do here. Berry does also, though he says that he prefers the term "incipient ternary." Green distinguishes between "sectional rounded binary" and continuous "rounded binary," the former being our binary/ternary, the latter our rounded binary. Kostka and Payne offer a curiously restricted definition which seems to rule out an extended reprise but includes the "balanced binary" form as a possibility.

[EXERCISE I.18]

EXAMPLE 3.9 Rounded binary form

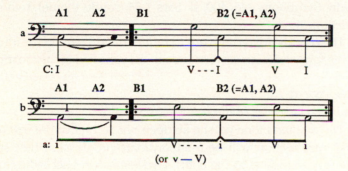

Exercises for Part I

For each assignment below, work out a complete bass-line sketch. Scores are included where necessary. Solutions for several exercises are given in an appendix at the end of the book. A list of additional suggestions for analysis (Assignments I.10-21) is keyed to commonly used music anthologies.

Assignment I.1

Chorale "Jesu, meine Freude" in J. S. Bach's setting (from the motet of the same name; no. 263 in the 371 Chorales). This setting is used at both beginning and end of the motet. The first verse is used here.

The chorales in assignments I.1-3 are written in an ancient design referred to as "bar-form." This design is distinct from the binary forms and has a completely different historical origin, but we can use the same structural bass patterns, nevertheless. The A-section of a bar-form is called the *Stollen* and normally ends on the tonic. Thus, we can use the model of the simply binary (tonic), with this caveat: a dominant prolongation in the beginning of the B-section (the *Abgesang*) is no more likely than a number of other possibilities. If the dominant is prolonged, then the sketch should have two open-note groups (I-V-I) overall; otherwise, it will probably have only one.

In this setting, use one structural group and treat the motion in the B-section as arpeggiation through the tonic triad (from 1 in bar 6 to 3 in bar 8 to 5 and 8 in bar 11). Expect that III will be prominent, as in most compositions in the minor key. A solution appears in the appendix.

Assignment I.2

Chorale "Wie schön leuchtet der Morgenstern" in J. S. Bach's setting (371 Chorales, no. 278). The cantata from which this was taken has been lost. The first verse is shown here.

See the note on bar-form above. Again use one open-note group overall. Arpeggiation plays a role in the first phrase. Use unfolding for E-A# in the final phrase. A solution appears in the appendix.

Assignment I.3

Chorale "Nun danket alle Gott" in J. S. Bach's setting (371 Chorales, no. 32). The cantata from which this was taken has been lost.

See the note on bar-form above. For this setting, use two structural open-note groups, because the first two phrases of "B" are best read as prolongations of the dominant. A subdominant bass arpeggiation (I-IV-I) is the basis of the first phrase. This chorale setting is included as an exercise in interpreting a highly embellished bass line.

Assignment I.4

Haydn, Symphony No. 100, II, bars 1-36 (rondo theme), two-stave reduction.

The repeats are written out to reflect Haydn's re-orchestrations, but the formal design corresponds to the rounded binary form.

Assignment I.5

Schubert, *Die schöne Müllerin*, "Morgengruß."

The first bass tone will be an open note (♩) , but the rest of the piano introduction will be a subordinate progression (not so the piano's little codetta at the end!). Divide the form according to the structure of the text. The resulting design will be similar to the instrumental rounded binary form.

Assignment I.6

Schumann, Album for the Young, op. 68, no. 14, "A Short Study."

First complete the chordal reduction begun in Ex. 1.36. Then place the bass-line sketch below, with correct alignment. Use one structural I-V-I group in bars 1-16 and one in bars 17 to the end.

Assignment I.7

Chopin, Prelude in B Minor, op. 28, no. 6 .

The techniques here are similar to those in Ex. 1.29 (Beethoven, op. 14, no. 2, I, end of the exposition). Your sketch should have one structural I-V-I group. Treat bars 18 to the first beat of 21 as the expansion of an unfolded third G down to E.

Assignment I.8

Mozart, Symphony No. 36, III, Menuet and Trio.

Analyze the Menuet and the Trio separately. The first bass tone of the Menuet is a prefix. Most of the many thirds in both Menuet and Trio are probably better notated with slurs than with unfolding symbols, but a few are appropriately shown with the latter. Also consult Chapter 3 before working these out: the Menuet is best assigned to the simple binary form (tonic), despite, or perhaps because of, its curious "inverted" reprise; the trio is a straightforward binary/ternary form with embellishment in the reprise.

Assignment I.9

Brahms, "Maienkätzchen," op. 107, No. 4.

The piano introduction provides a dominant "prefix" to the first open-note I (bar 3). The formal design has two parts, as if two verses of a strophic song; use two open-note groups. The piano's interlude between the verses is a foreground feature—use closed notes. The structural cadence (final open-note V-I) should follow the voice part: The piano's coda is subordinate to (prolongs) the final open-note I. A solution appears in the appendix.

Assignment I.10

Write an essay/outline describing as precisely as you can the meaning and function of every symbol in the bass of one of the following figures from *Free Composition*: Fig. 68 (Schubert); 96,4 (Brahms); 110,3 (Chopin); 152,4 (Bach); or 153,3 (Chopin).

Assignment I.11

Write an essay explaining in detail (and, if appropriate, criticizing) Felix Salzer's bass-line analysis of Brahms, Symphony No. 3, first movement (*Structural Hearing*, Fig. 503; text commentary in vol. 1, 247-48).

Assignment I.12

Work out a detailed bass-line sketch of one of the Chopin Preludes, then write a short essay relating tonal and formal design. If a published analysis exists for the Prelude you have chosen, you may optionally compare your reading with the bass of the published analysis.

Assignment I.13

Work out bass-line sketches for two Bach dances of the same name (for example, two gavottes), then write a short essay comparing tonal and formal design. Options: Dances or dance movements by Lully, Corelli, D'Anglebert, Handel, or Couperin; or two Classic-period menuets.

Assignment I.14

Work out a bass-line sketch for variation set by Mozart, Haydn, or Beethoven, then write a short essay comparing the motions of the bass in the theme and its variations.

ADDITIONAL SUGGESTIONS FOR ANALYSIS:

The list below is arranged chronologically by period, not in order of difficulty.

I.15. Brief, tonally complete examples organized by chord vocabulary, as in Arlin et al, *Music Sources*, second edition, make excellent short exercises during the study of Chapter 1. We suggest, for example, working out one or two examples in each of the first fourteen sections of *Music Sources*.

I.16. F. Couperin, *Les baricades mistérieuses*, in Burkhart, *Anthology for Musical Analysis*, fourth edition. A more challenging problem. Using the sketch in Chapter 3 as your basis, do a detailed analysis of the bass.

I.17. J. S. Bach, setting of chorale "Wachet auf!" in Wennerstrom, *Anthology of Musical Structure and Style*. A large bar-form chorale that has many features in common with "Wie schön leuchtet der Morgenstern."

I.18. J. S. Bach, setting of chorale "Ach, bleib bei uns, Herr Jesu Christ" in Wennerstrom, *Anthology of Musical Structure and*

Style. A four-phrase chorale with a cadence to the tonic in phrase two. Use one open-note group. Not difficult.

I.19.   J. S. Bach, French Suite in E Major, Gavotte in Wennerstrom, *Anthology of Musical Structure and Style.* The structural return of the tonic occurs in bar 16. This is one of those cases in which the tonic return is clear enough, but the form category is not: Is bar 16 a reprise (with the two right-hand voices inverted)? And, if so, is it a reprise of A1 or A2?

I.20.   Mozart, Sonata for Piano and Violin, K. 404, II, in Arlin et al., *Music Sources*, second edition. Though the music is embellished, this is actually a simple problem in binary/ternary design, with a very limited chord vocabulary.

I.21.   Beethoven, Piano Sonata, op. 109, III, theme, in Arlin et al., *Music Sources*, second edition. Simple binary (dominant) with a rather active bass. Compare your sketch with the bass in Forte and Gilbert's analysis.

I.22.   Beethoven, Piano Sonata in E major, op. 14, no. 1, II in Wennerstrom, *Anthology of Musical Structure and Style;* also in Burkhart, *Anthology for Musical Analysis*, fourth edition. Do the menuet/scherzo (Allegretto) but not its trio, which is tonally incomplete—or, for a challenge, do the entire movement. In the Allegretto, the traditional repeat signs are missing; you must make judgments for yourself about the formal design. Two hints: motion toward the dominant in bars 31-32 is important structurally, as is what follows in bar 33.

I.23.   Schubert, Waltzes, op. 9, nos. 14 and 29 in Wennerstrom, *Anthology of Musical Structure and Style.* Small but interesting problems in chromaticism.

I.24.   Schubert, *Die schöne Müllerin*, "Der Müller und der Bach" in Wennerstrom, *Anthology of Musical Structure and Style.* A longer piece, but not difficult (for a bass-line sketch at least!) if you treat each verse of the text as corresponding to a structural unit of the music.

I.25.   Schubert, Moments musicaux, op. 94, no. 6 in Arlin et al., *Music Sources*, second edition; also in Burkhart, *Anthology for Musical Analysis*, fourth edition. A challenging problem involving chromatic mediants in an extended binary/ternary design. The trio is also written in a binary/ternary form.

I.26.   Chopin, Mazurka, op. 7, no. 1, in Burkhart, *Anthology for Musical Analysis*, fourth edition. Treat this as if it were a rondo: "A" in bars 1-12, written-out repeat in 13-24, "B" in 25-32, reprise in 33-44, "C" in 45-53, reprise in 54 ff. Except for its length, not a difficult problem.

I.27.   Brahms, Waltzes, op. 39, no. 3, in Arlin et al., *Music Sources*, second edition. Simple binary (non-tonic), but what is the degree that closes "A"? (Treat that chord as the V of a later-level I-V-I group). Use one structural open-note group overall. A more difficult problem than it may seem.

EXAMPLE I.1 Chorale "Jesu, meine Freude" in J. S. Bach's setting (from Motet No. 3)

EXAMPLE I.2 Chorale "Wie schön leuchtet der Morgenstern" in J. S. Bach's setting (371 Chorales, No. 278)

EXAMPLE I.3 Chorale "Nun danket alle Gott" in J. S. Bach's setting (371 Chorales, No. 32)

EXAMPLE I.4 Haydn, Symphony No. 100, II, bars 1-36 (rondo theme)

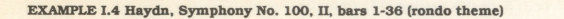

EXAMPLE I.5 Schubert, Die schöne Müllerin, "Morgengruß"

1. Gu- ten Mor-gen, schö-ne Mül-le-rin! wo steckst du gleich das Köpf-chen hin, als

wär dir was ge-sche-hen? Ver-drießt dich denn mein Gruß so schwer? ver-stört dich denn mein Blick so sehr? So

muß ich wie-der ge-hen, so muß ich wie-der ge-hen, wie-der ge-hen.

EXAMPLE I.6 Schumann, Album for the Young, op. 68, no. 14, "A Short Study"

EXAMPLE I.6 continued

EXAMPLE I.7 Chopin, Prelude in B Minor, op. 28, no. 6

EXAMPLE I.8 Mozart, Symphony No. 36, III, Menuet and Trio

Menuetto

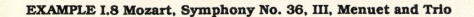

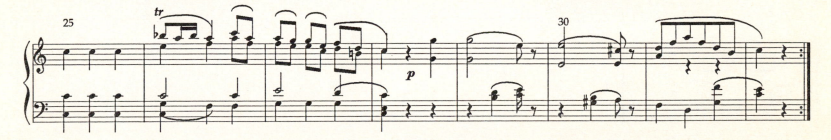

EXAMPLE I.8 continued

Trio

Minuetto D.C.

EXAMPLE I.9 Brahms, "Maienkätzchen," op. 107, no. 4

Chapter 4: Preliminary: Informal Introduction to Upper-Voice Analysis

A tone moves to any other in one of three ways: by step, by leap, or obliquely. From these derive the three main methods of linear motion (in bass or upper parts): lines, arpeggiations, and stationary or recurrent tones. All other melodic motions are combinations or specialized variants of these three. In this chapter, we will make a brief and informal study of a method to analyze the principal linear motions of the upper voices. In the following chapters, this approach will be formalized; that is, it will be brought into line with Schenkerian concepts and notation.

To carry out an analysis using this method, follow these steps:

1. First isolate a formal unit (phrase or period).

2. Locate and circle the initial tone, final tone, and highest tone. (It is often helpful to write out all the melodic tones as unstemmed noteheads; include bar lines.) If the first tone is an anacrusis or pick-up note, the first accented tone may be taken; if the highest tone is a simple embellishing tone (such as the d''' in the Schubert waltz of Ex. 1.3), the next lower or prominently placed tone may be taken; if the final tone does not appear to be the last structural tone, choose the latter instead. Make decisions based on what seems most workable or musically convincing at the time—remember that this procedure is informal.

3. Try to chart the essential motion between the initial and highest tones, and between the highest and final tones. Give preference to a single line (for example, if the highest note is g'' and the last is d'', look for a line descending from g'' to d''). This line may have repetitions of tones or segments, may have neighbor-note figures attached, and may be chromatic or diatonic. The second segment (from highest tones to last) will almost always be a line; if so,

connect its notes with a beam. The first segment (from first tone to highest), on the other hand, may be a line, an arpeggiated figure, or a combination of both. Arpeggiations should consist of tones of the *tonic* triad (or local tonic of a region), ascending. Be wary of descending arpeggiations: they will rarely be of consequence in a voice-leading graph.

Register (octave) changes may be included, but avoid them unless they are obviously needed. Some cognizance may be taken of harmony, but at this stage do *not* try to fit every melodic tone to an underlying chord.

4. Mark the resulting figures using any convenient means, perhaps with stemmed closed notes and a slur, or with beamed closed notes.

5. An optional additional step is to try to locate linear fragments in the inner voices. These will not usually run consistently from beginning to end, nor are they likely to be coordinated, note for note, with the principal upper-voice motions.

The first eight bars of Ex. 1.12 (Haydn Menuet) will serve as our first illustration of this method. These bars constitute a two-phrase period which is also the A-section of a rounded binary form. To begin, the two four-bar phrases will be considered separately.

Ex. 4.1 reproduces all the right-hand notes in bars 1-4. The first tone is c''; the highest tone is c'''; the final tone is e''. These are circled. From c'' to c''' an ascending figure which is partly arpeggio, partly step, may be easily traced (see the first part of Ex. 4.2), but from c''' to e'' we have only the undesirable direct descending arpeggio c'''-g''-e'' with a neighbor figure appended, e''-f''-e''. Another alternative is more satisfying: a line descending from g" to e". The status of c''' is thus somewhat uncertain—we will find that g", not c''', is the principal melodic tone of these bars; c''' is what is called a *cover tone* —literally, a note "covering," or moving above, the principal melodic voice. The cover tone is a very common phenomenon and is discussed further in Chapters 5 and 6.

EXAMPLE 4.1 Haydn, Menuet in C, bars 1-4

EXAMPLE 4.2 Haydn, Menuet in C, bars 1-4, melodic analysis

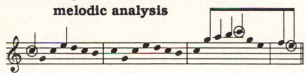

Our attention is to be focused on the principal upper voice, but it is worth observing that inner voices are often easily traced from tones of an arpeggiation figure. In bar 1, for example, we might have chosen d" to follow c", but the grace note suggests that d" follows better from e". Thus, c" has a neighbor note (c"-b'-c") and e" moves in a line (e"-e"-c"). These figures are repeated in bars 2-3.

In bars 4-8 (Ex. 4.3), d" is the first tone, a" the highest, and d" the last. As shown, the first two are adjacent, and a line is easily traced from a" to d" at the end.

EXAMPLE 4.3 Haydn, Menuet in C, bars 4-8, melodic analysis

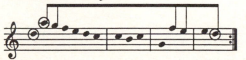

The two phrases may be combined and the resulting period analyzed as a single unit: see Ex. 4.4. Now, c" is the first tone, c''' the highest, and d" the last, but we substitute g" for c''' for reasons

discussed above. The line ending the first phrase is now subordinate, as is the first part of the line from a" in the second phrase.

EXAMPLE 4.4 Haydn, Menuet in C, bars 1-8, melodic analysis

This method is by no means sufficient for all compositions, nor should it be assumed that the resulting lines will always be fundamental lines or even deep middleground figures. They are as likely to consist of fragments of more than one actual voice-leading part. As we have said earlier, the upper parts can be very complex, with two or more separate voice-leading strands running through a single melodic line (and often appearing and disappearing). *It is only when the principal upper-voice motions are coordinated with the bass-line sketch that we have criteria for separating and judging these elements according to the contexts of the different structural levels.* As it happens (conveniently), our informal melodic analysis and the bass-line sketch of the Haydn Menuet may be fitted together without too much difficulty (see Ex. 4.5). We must wait for certain other techniques to be discussed in Chapters 5 and 6 before we can display the upper voices in formal Schenkerian notation.

EXAMPLE 4.5 Haydn, Menuet in C, bars 1-8, melodic analysis and bass-line sketch combined

Our second analysis problem is "The Star-Spangled Banner," which is reproduced without text at the bottom of Ex. 4.6. In this melody, we can isolate three long phrases of eight bars each (1-8, 9-16, 17-24). The second staff (from the bottom) analyzes each of these phrases separately. In phrase 1, the lowest note (and also the last) is small b♭, and the highest is d", the principal melody note, as the stepwise motion downward in bar 5 makes clear. We might have considered the d" to be a cover tone over an essential b♭' (the next tonic-chord tone down), but only neighboring motion can be read from that b♭'. Normally, we prefer lines over neighbor-note figures as essential melodic patterns. In most circumstances, extended neighbor-note motion will embellish (or prolong) notes of a structurally more significant line.

In phrase 2, the first note touches on d" again, but the highest note is f". Since there is linear motion from the f", we would normally pick that as principal melodic tone, but here we can allow ourselves to be influenced by changes we would clearly have to make when we combine the phrases for a complete analysis of the melody. Thus, f" is a cover tone; d" remains the principal melodic tone, but a line descends from f" down to d" (referred to as an *upper-third-line*), and the final note of the phrase, f', is isolated as an inner voice. (Our reading is, admittedly, also influenced by the very familiar harmonization of this melody, so that we have ignored a possible continuation of the line from b♭' to a', g', and f' in bars 13 to 16. In any case, even from a purely melodic perspective, the g' functions exclusively as a neighbor note to a'.)

The final phrase begins from b♭', continues with a rather elaborate embellishment of a neighbor note figure, b♭'-c"-b♭', reaches the cover tone f" quickly, and then closes with two third-lines, one rising from b♭' to d", the other descending d"-c"-b♭'.

The two upper staves of Ex. 4.6 go a step beyond our method in this chapter to show formal Schenkerian notation. The first includes every note of the melody and is labelled "foreground 2"; the uppermost staff has fewer details and is labelled "foreground 1" (remember: the lower the number, the earlier in the composing-out process for levels with the same name).

EXAMPLE 4.6 "The Star-Spangled Banner," melodic analysis

Our third example is the British national anthem, "God Save the Queen," known in the United States as "America" (see Ex. 4.7). Again, the melody is shown at the bottom, with an informal analysis above it. This melody consists of three phrases, bars 1-6, 7-10, 11-14, with the last two closely linked. In the first phrase, motion is stepwise, to and from g'. The highest note is c'', but it is obviously a neighbor note to b'; thus, we have two third-lines, one rising g'-a'-b', the other descending b'-a'-g'. Following our rule, we give preference to the latter and connect its notes with a beam.

The second phrase begins with its highest note and, through a sequential pattern, spills over into the first note of the next phrase, b'. This final phrase leads upward as high as e'', but this is an escape tone, the primary note being the tonic-chord tone d'' before it. Thus, we have an ascending line, b'-c''-d'', and a structural descending line, d''-c''-b'-a'-g'.

Overall, then, this melody can be analyzed as in the upper staves of Ex. 4.7, which are written in formal Schenkerian notation. The g'

and b' of the first phrase are part of an arpeggiated ascent to d'', the fundamental tone 5̂, which is prolonged by further lines until the descent at the end.

A note about counterpoint: In the strictest Schenkerian pedagogy, species counterpoint is learned first, followed by (or concurrent with) figured bass, and finally harmony, which leads directly to Schenkerian analysis. (See David Beach, "Schenker's Theories: A Pedagogical View," in Beach, ed., *Aspects of Schenkerian Theory*, pp. 1-38.) Our position, based on our teaching experience, is that a secure knowledge of traditional voice-leading or part-writing principles gives requisite skills for good analytic work, although some familiarity with species counterpoint gives one an advantage. For the Schenkerian specialist, an understanding of species counterpoint is a necessity. On species counterpoint, see Chapter 2 of Forte and Gilbert; the early chapters of *Structural Hearing*; Felix Salzer and Carl Schachter, *Counterpoint in Composition* (New York 1969); or Peter Westergaard, *Introduction to Tonal Theory* (New York 1975). Schenker's own two-volume *Counterpoint* (1911, 1922) has recently been published in translation (New York 1987).

EXAMPLE 4.7 "God Save the Queen," melodic analysis

Chapter 5: Three Analysis Narratives

This chapter opens with a short account of an analysis which shows, albeit somewhat simplistically, how we may add a soprano, or principal upper part, to a bass-line sketch. This account considers all soprano-voice tones, but it is actually concerned primarily with the problem of choosing the first tone of the fundamental line. The second analysis narrative begins with discussion of a five-stage procedure for the construction of a set of analytic graphs; both second and third narratives are demonstrations of the application of this procedure. A final section, "Priorities for Analysis of the Upper Parts," offers some guidelines and rules of thumb for analysis work.

In general, the procedures we espouse are, first, to forge through to the background as quickly as possible, informally testing alternatives along the way, without attempting to produce detailed graphs at any level; then, once the interpretation of the background and the first middleground is secure, to work one's way in a leisurely and careful manner back out toward the foreground.

J. S. BACH, SETTING OF THE CHORALE "DU FRIEDENSFÜRST, HERR JESU CHRIST"

This chorale setting is the closing movement of Cantata No. 67 (No. 42 in the 371 Chorales). The text used is the first stanza of the hymn. Bach's setting begins with 3̂ harmonized by the tonic chord, but the highest note in the first phrase is e″ (5̂)—see Ex. 5.1, which includes the score and a bass-line sketch. A quick scan of the other phrases shows e″ once again above c♯″ in phrase 2, but the highest tone thereafter is d″ (bar 8). The B-section, which is the *Abgesang* of a bar-form, has no tonic-chord tone higher than we find in the A-section (the *Stollen*). Therefore, we can rule out the extended initial ascent which is common in chorales. (Note: An initial ascent is a middleground ascending figure, line or arpeggio, that leads to the first note of the fundamental line. The tonic-chord arpeggio leading to g″ in the Haydn Menuet discussed in Chapter 4 is an example of initial ascent. For more information, see Chapter 6 below.)

EXAMPLE 5.1 Chorale "Du Friedensfürst, Herr Jesu Christ" in J. S. Bach's setting; score and bass sketch

Turning back to the first phrase, we find that the bass analysis shows a network of mostly stepwise patterns about the tonic degree. The tonic appears three times, always in root position, and in every case the soprano tone is c#''. The e'', on the other hand, is harmonized by V⁶, in this context a passing chord, not a functional sonority. All this evidence suggests that c#'' is the first tone of the fundamental line, and that the apparent line from e'' (e''-d''-c#'') represents boundary play: see Ex. 5.2.

EXAMPLE 5.2 "Du Friedensfürst," bars 1-4, chorale melody matched to bass sketch

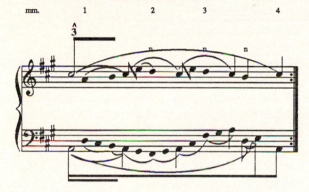

The soprano, then, mirrors the bass: figures revolving about c#'', but moving for the most part in contrary motion to the bass. This smooth but supple counterpoint of the outer parts, along with the strictly diatonic setting (until bar 6), very limited ornamentation, and recurring root-position tonic with c#'', should not be overlooked as expressive of the sense of "Du Friedensfürst"—"You Prince of Peace."[1]

---

[1] An alternate interpretation of the soprano is possible: $\hat{3}$-$\hat{4}$-($\hat{3}$-$\hat{2}$)-$\hat{3}$, where $\hat{4}$ is a neighbor note to the $\hat{3}$ at the end, and the $\hat{3}$-$\hat{2}$ in parentheses is part of a 3-line embellishing the $\hat{4}$. See *Free Composition*, Figs. 22,b (Schumann); 119,8 (Beethoven), to see how such an argument could be justified, even though it contradicts the bass support for the second $\hat{3}$.

But we also need to consider the e'' in the second phrase, since it is possible that c#'' in bar 1-2 might be a prolonged tone of initial ascent. Once again e'' is not harmonized by the root-position tonic chord, but by I⁶, and the line which leads from it down to c#'' is harmonized by a relatively weak subdominant embellishing motion, I⁶-IV⁶-I. It is true, on the other hand, that the contrapuntal pattern created by the two tonic chords in bar 2 (Ex. 5.3) is often used as a way of harmonizing an initial ascent to $\hat{5}$.

EXAMPLE 5.3 Parallel tenths in an initial ascent to $\hat{5}$

In the last bars of the chorale, a line d''-c#''-b'-a' might be linked to the e'' in bar 2, but is this musically convincing? The d'' in its context sounds very much like a neighbor note to c#'' and not at all like a passing tone from e''. Our choice for the first tone of the structural line must be $\hat{3}$. Analysis of the fundamental structure and remaining soprano-bass counterpoint may be worked out as in Ex. 5.4.

A rule of thumb may be derived from this: When in doubt about $\hat{3}$ or $\hat{5}$, choose $\hat{3}$; and, analogously, when in doubt about $\hat{5}$ or $\hat{8}$, choose $\hat{5}$. Obviously then, you should expect to find more fundamental lines from $\hat{3}$ than from $\hat{5}$ or $\hat{8}$. The composition discussed in the next section below also has a fundamental line from $\hat{3}$. The Introduction offered an example of a line from $\hat{5}$ in Weber's "Leise, leise, fromme Weise"; the final section of this chapter will focus on a piece with a fundamental line from $\hat{8}$.

EXAMPLE 5.4 "Du Friedensfürst," foreground graph

J. S. BACH, WELL-TEMPERED CLAVIER, VOL. 1, PRELUDE IN C MAJOR

Reduction, or reductive analysis, refers to the analytic process working essentially inward from the score to the fundamental structure. Composing-out, or generative analysis, is linked closely to the compositional process, as Schenker interprets it, working from the fundamental structure outward toward the score. We may take reduction to be the path of "discovering" the fundamental structure, of initial study for performance or understanding; composing-out, on the other hand, is the path of composition and of a more advanced or complete understanding. The reciprocal nature of reductive and generative analysis may be shown with the following figure:

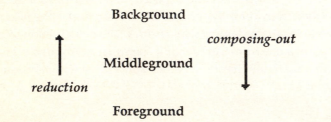

A complete and adequate Schenkerian analysis of a composition, therefore, involves both reduction and a reading of composing-out, but the emphasis must be placed mainly on the latter, since a final set of graphs is first and foremost an elucidation of the composing-out process.

We may isolate five stages in the creation of a complete set of analysis graphs. First, construct a bass-line sketch. In an essay in *Das Meisterwerk in der Musik*, vol. 2, Schenker himself stressed the importance of this:

> To make discovery of the *Urlinie* progression easier, I suggest locating that first arpeggiation by means of which the bass develops the fundamental tonic triad....Find its dividing dominant and try to determine the path to that dominant....Only then will it be possible to understand the many other bass arpeggiations as...subordinate entities in the service of that first tonic-triad arpeggiation; and one will be able to distinguish the various meanings of the many lines in the composing-out of the upper parts and arrive at the true *Urlinie*. (21-22)

Second, determine the first note of the fundamental line by going through the process described in the discussion of "Du Friedensfürst" above (perhaps beginning with an informal melodic analysis of the kind discussed in Chapter 4), by matching some of the patterns of the soprano with the bass-line sketch, and by examining closely the opening phrase(s) and the final structural cadence.

Third, proceed with the "formal" construction of the graphs, starting with the background. Decide how many levels will be included. If you need more than three, the extra levels should usually be middlegrounds. Use more than one foreground only if the graphs are particularly intended to concentrate on details. The *Urlinietafel* of *Five Graphic Music Analyses* is a specialized foreground graph which mixes structural analysis with actual score notation of some events. (An *Urlinietafel* [literally, "Urlinie-table" or "graph"] is easily recognized because it includes bar-lines. We will call the *Urlinietafel* a "score foreground.")

In a complete set of graphs, the fundamental structure may be placed either at the top or at the bottom. We prefer the method used in *Five Graphic Music Analyses*, in which the fundamental structure appears at the top and later levels below it (or on successive pages when necessary). Since readers of Western languages are accustomed to reading from the top of the page down, this arrangement gives a good parallel to the process of composing-out.

Make sure that all the content of any level is present in all succeeding levels, and be sure to align all the graphs vertically.

Fourth, when the foreground graph is completed, read the set of graphs in reverse—that is, from foreground to background, or in "reductive" order—to make sure that there are no gaps in the logical sequence from one level to the next or failures to represent your interpretation accurately.

Fifth, if appropriate, add text commentary to suit your purpose.

The formal design of the Prelude in C Major from the first volume of the Well-Tempered Clavier, like that of many Baroque preludes, follows overall harmonic patterning rather than predictable phrase groups. From the score (Ex. 5.5a[2]) and even more clearly in the slightly reduced four-voice version above it (Ex. 5.5b), the motions of the bass emerge, and we can chart them in a bass-line sketch (see Ex. 5.6, and the bass staff of Ex. 5.5,1).

The next step—choosing the first note of the fundamental line—poses no problems. The $\hat{3}$ appears immediately as e'', which is embellished by a neighbor note f''. In bars 6 and following, linear motion clearly continues downward from this e''. The a'' in bar 5 and g'' in bar 7 are among the most simple examples of cover tones; that is, notes that lie above the main melodic motion. Note in particular that g'' is left entirely by itself in the upper register, with no linear continuation of any kind.

By matching upper-voice motions to the middleground-level view of the bass line, we can create the elements of a middleground graph (see Ex. 5.5,3). The uppermost voice, or soprano, at first follows the bass in parallel tenths, then interlocks two unfoldings, c''-e' and b'-f'. The prolongation of the fundamental note above the first beamed I-V-I group (bars 1-19) thus includes a register transfer of e'' to e'. The only remaining essential motion in the Prelude is the descent of the fundamental line itself.

At this point we need to consider the appropriate number of levels to use in the final set of graphs. Determining that number is most easily accomplished by creating and examining a first middleground graph (that is, Ex. 5.5,4) and asking how much additional detail is needed to reach the foreground, or, conversely, how much detail must be removed to reach the background. Our middleground graph has one first-order diminution (the neighbor note figure E-F-E that emerges when we "correct" the register transfer to e'), and two second-order diminutions (the third-line downward to

---

[2] Though this prelude is always printed with the arpeggiations written out in sixteenth notes, one manuscript version simply shows the underlying harmonies; this version was used here. Since it is not complete, we have been obliged to add a few chords.

the inner-voice c′ and the interlocked unfoldings); plus inner-voice motions. If we chose to show the composing-out process in great detail and very carefully (in the manner of many of Cube's graphs), we would write a background, foreground, and one middleground for each layer of diminutions (first-order, second-order, and so on). Mostly for the sake of economy of presentation, we will use three middlegrounds and a foreground, without a separate background, since the fundamental structure is plainly visible in the first middleground, Ex. 5.5,4. Exs. 5.5,3; 5.5,2; and 5.5,1 are second middleground, third middleground, and foreground, respectively. Exs. 5.5,a and 5.5,b may be regarded as score foregrounds.

In general, begin with the assumption that a set of analysis graphs for a composition will have three levels: background or first middleground, middleground, and foreground. If these do not seem enough and the object of the analysis is to show the stages of composing-out, then add more middlegrounds; if the object is to study motivic detail, add another foreground. In other words, the number of levels and sublevels depends on the composition, but also on the needs of the analysis itself.

As our work with this Prelude suggests, you may use a Middleground I level as the deepest level in a set of graphs (particularly if there is an interruption figure or first-order register transfer (coupling)), but be certain that you label the graph correctly: "Middleground 1," *not* "Background." This is a distinction which, unfortunately, is too often ignored even in the scholarly literature. Strictly speaking, the background may contain *only* the fundamental structure; that is, the fundamental line and its bass arpeggiation(s). Even the interruption, despite its open notes, belongs to the middleground. The only exception to this rule is instanced by Schenker's reading of this Prelude in *Five Graphic Music Analyses*: inner voices in closed notes fill out the harmonies and effect an 8-7 motion above V.

Finally, check the graphs by reading in a reductive mode (from the foreground in). This step is mainly for the purpose of insuring that the foreground and middleground do not contradict one another. Then we can add any commentary we wish, either as annotations to the graphs or as a separate text. Here we will omit commentary in favor of the suggestion that you will find it interesting and instructive to compare the reading in Ex. 5.5 with Schenker's analysis in *Five Graphic Music Analyses*. Cube translates this reading (with some notational changes) into a striking "3D" rendering in *The Book of the Musical Artwork*. Forte and Gilbert have a version in their own style of notation (p. 202). Also consult William Drabkin's article, "A Lesson in Analysis from Heinrich Schenker: The C Major Prelude from Bach's Well-Tempered Clavier, Book I," *Music Analysis* 4 (1985): 241-258.

EXAMPLE 5.6 J. S. Bach, The Well-Tempered Clavier, Vol. 1, Prelude in C Major, bass-line sketch

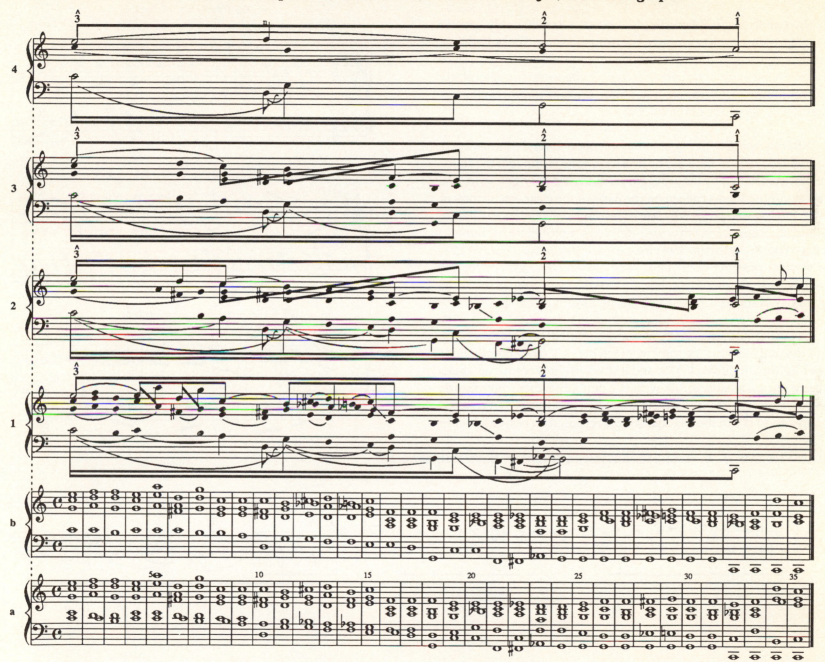

EXAMPLE 5.9 J. S. Bach, Invention in G Major, bars 1-9

The Invention in G Major (Ex. 5.7) poses a considerably greater challenge than any piece we have encountered so far. The polyphonic texture suggests a number of voice-leading strands which may not be obvious in the score, and the bass is complex because it is melodically active throughout. On the other hand, we can take comfort in the fact that there is very little chromaticism.

After listening to or playing the Invention several times, inspect the analyzed bass in Ex. 5.8. The first tonic tone is implied: the chord is plainly presented by the arpeggiated motive in the right hand. The first open-note V was chosen on the basis of the clear establishment of the dominant key region by bar 10, leading to the cadence in bar 14, the end of section A in a fairly well-defined simple binary (dominant) design. The second open-note I may come either in bar 17 or bar 22—the earliest possible occurrence was chosen here. Except for the extensive use of unfolded thirds (derived from the subject), the remainder of the bass-line sketch has no unusual features.

Given the bass-line sketch, we can assume that the first note of the fundamental line must be somewhere in bars 1-7. The arpeggiations of bar 1 offer four tones: $\hat{1}$, $\hat{3}$, $\hat{5}$, and $\hat{8}$ (Ex. 5.9). Only from $\hat{8}$ (g″) does subsequent voice leading follow: first, a double neighbor-note figure, then, a leisurely descent to $\hat{3}$ (b′) in bar 7. At that point, g″ is recovered and moves to f♯″ in the next bar (this is repeated an octave lower in

EXAMPLE 5.8 J. S. Bach, Invention in G Major, bass-line sketch

EXAMPLE 5.7 J. S. Bach, Invention in G Major, score

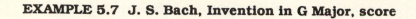

the following two bars). All this suggests that $\hat{8}$ is the best candidate for the first tone of the fundamental line. (The only possible alternative to $\hat{8}$ might be $\hat{3}$, first reached as b'' in bar 11. This moves immediately to $\hat{2}$ in bar 12, which would create an interruption figure. A descent could occur, then, in bars 29-30 or 31-32. This is, however, an unsatisfactory interpretation, the most compelling reason being that this $\hat{3}$ plays almost no role in the voice leading of the great majority of the piece.)

The fundamental line from $\hat{8}$ is not common (some Schenkerians even doubt its legitimacy as an fundamental line construct). The next step, then, is to verify the line by determining (1) whether the remaining tones of the line can be located; and (2) whether the closing cadence fits clearly into the structure thus produced. As Ex. 5.10 shows, the motion $\hat{7}$-$\hat{6}$-$\hat{5}$ supported by harmonies in the dominant key

EXAMPLE 5.10 J. S. Bach, Invention in G Major, bars 10-13

EXAMPLE 5.11 J. S. Bach, Invention in G Major, final bars

region occurs in the cadence of section A. This is the ideal placement and support for this part of the divided octave-line.

In Ex. 5.11 is an interpretation of the closing bars. The "false" descent of bars 29-30 is repeated an octave lower over strong supporting harmonies and supplies the $\hat{3}$-$\hat{2}$-$\hat{1}$ conclusion of the fundamental line. The remaining tone—$\hat{4}$ (c'')—may be found in several places between bars 14 and 31, notably in the long-held trilled note of bars 20-21, but the tone that was chosen (in the upper octave in bar 28; lower octave in bar 30) is the $\hat{4}$ immediately connected to $\hat{3}$ in the descent. This seemed the most convincing choice, in part because of the continued emphasis on $\hat{5}$ in bars 26-27.

The fundamental structure produced by the steps described above appears at the top of Ex. 5.12. (Note that the V-I in bars 30-31 was changed from closed notes in the bass-line sketch to open notes: Tonic or dominant roots supporting tones of the fundamental line are shown with open notes; all other supporting tones are closed.)

We will assume that the remaining stages of composing-out can be represented with two levels, one middleground and one foreground. The content of the background should first be copied into these two levels, with all three aligned vertically. This insures that the complete background content will also appear in all later levels, as it must. Next the main features of the bass-line sketch should be copied into the middleground graph, and the entire bass-line sketch into the foreground graph.

The motions of the middleground and foreground can now be coordinated with those of the bass-line sketch, in a manner similar to the coordinating of structural bass arpeggiation and fundamental line. Probably the most comfortable way to do this is to work simultaneously on middleground and foreground in specific passages; for example, bars 2-10 (or between the first $\hat{8}$ and the appearance of $\hat{7}$). (The controlling feature of bar 1 must be an initial ascent—obviously, the arpeggiation of the tonic triad from g' to g''.)

The remainder of the graphs may be worked out along these lines. The results appear in Ex. 5.12. After checking the graphs by reading from the foreground in, we can add any appropriate text commentary. In this case, the present narrative serves that purpose. One might add brief descriptive notes for each level, in the manner of Cube (see Exercises for Part II for three samples), or comment on the many striking motivic features of this piece.

EXAMPLE 5.10 J. S. Bach, Invention in G Major, analytic graphs (background/middleground/foreground)

PRIORITIES FOR ANALYSIS OF THE UPPER PARTS

It can be a great help in the analysis process to have constantly in mind the priorities for motions of the upper voices. In the bass, decisions are made relatively easy because patterns generally coincide with functional hierarchies, but in the upper parts, the task is not so simple. Invariably the most difficult problem in carrying out an analysis is reconciling the clearly observable features of the score with the limited number of abstract models Schenker provides. In practical terms, this is the problem of interpreting the middleground. One is inclined to equate "prominence" with "significance," yet, as we have seen in the case of cover tones, these two do not necessarily coincide.

More specific guidelines:

1. The patterns of the upper parts (or at least the principal upper part) must coincide with the bass patterns *at the same level of structure*. This means that a first-middleground bass figure must have a corresponding first-middleground upper-voice figure, and so on, through the several levels of structure (whether those levels are readily named or not).

   In Ex. 5.5,4 (Bach C-Major Prelude), for example, the harmonic cycle I-ii^7-V^7-I spanning bars 1-19 belongs to the first middleground motion; its corresponding upper voice is the neighbor-note motion e''-f''-e''. The first three bass tones, c'-small b-a, of Ex. 5.5,3 are accompanied by parallel tenths (the remainder of the passage is complicated by the interlocking unfoldings). In the foreground (Ex. 5.5,1), the opening c'-small b-c' of the bass moves with a neatly corresponding double-neighbor figure in the soprano: e''-f''-d''-e''.

2. The central problem in working out the background and first middleground is to locate the first tone of the fundamental line. Some aids to this end:

   a. Use the rule of thumb given earlier in this chapter: "When in doubt about $\hat{3}$ or $\hat{5}$, choose $\hat{3}$ (and, analogously, when in doubt about $\hat{5}$ or $\hat{8}$, choose $\hat{5}$)."

b. At the beginning of the piece, examine any rising figures. Assume that these represent an initial ascent; then pick the last or second last tonic-chord tone as the probable first note of the fundamental line. Next, apply these additional rules of thumb:

Ask from what note the voice leading follows in the early bars of the piece. Unless it is an element of an extended initial ascent pattern, this note will usually be the first tone of the fundamental line. Look ahead, for instance, at Ex. 6.1 (Handel, *Messiah*, Pastoral Symphony): a step-progression leads directly to g'', followed by a neighbor motion and descending third line(s). Also see Exs. 6.2 and 6.9 (Beethoven, Bagatelle, op. 119, no. 9). A simple but extended arpeggiation of the tonic triad leads to c''', from which a line immediately follows (c'''-b♭''-a''-g♯'').

In addition, look at the final cadence of the composition, specifically, at the shape of the descent in the principal upper part, as well as its harmonic support.

Finally, in difficult cases, it may be necessary to construct preliminary graphs with different fundamental lines—this will always provide a sufficient basis for a decision.

3. Analyze the formal design and choose an appropriate model. The interruption will be used in binary forms and related pieces; interruption or the large-scale neighbor note or mixture (chromatic neighbor note) will be used in three-part forms, etc. (Some of these models are discussed in Chapter 8.) Although there are many deviations from these models, they do provide some idea of typical patterns to look for in the different compositional genres.

4. Assume that interrupted lines will probably play an important role in the first or second middleground of most compositions of any size. (In the Bach G-Major Invention, as in all pieces with an octave line, division at $\hat{5}$ takes the place of an interrupted line.) Most of the pieces included in the Exercises for Part II employ interrupted lines in the first middleground; several have lower-level interruptions as well.

5. In the middleground and foreground, the upper parts in individual passages may often be analyzed using the list below (in order of preference):

a. A descending line that matches the main harmonic activity. Look ahead at Ex. 6.6, bars 1-8 (Schubert): A fifth line that matches a complete harmonic cycle in the bass.

b. (as good) An interrupted line.

c. A neighbor-note figure linked to the structural tone at the beginning of the passage (or possibly prolonged from a previous passage). See Ex. 5.5 (Bach). Also, Ex. II.12, bars 1-8, below (Chopin, Mazurka, op. 67, no. 3). A simple upbeat figure reaches the first tone of the fundamental line, $\hat{3}$ (e''), in bar 1. The harmonic motion in bars 1-8 is I-V$^6_5$/V-V^7-I. To the first I belongs the $\hat{3}$ (and a little foreground third-line, e''-d''-c''); to the V$^6_5$/V an implied $\hat{2}$ (d''); to the V^7, a regained e'' (bar 6) and either the $\hat{2}$ or both the $\hat{2}$ and $\hat{4}$ (d'' and f') as neighbor notes before the e'' is recovered in bar 8 (implied above, but actually present as e' in the left-hand afterbeats).

d. A held structural tone with moving inner parts (line, neighbor note, etc.) and/or boundary play. See Ex. 6.10, first phrase (J.S.Bach, setting of "Christ lag in Todesbanden"). The $\hat{5}$ (b') begins and ends the phrase. After the neighbor note a#', the motion is boundary play, the principal figure being the upper third-line d''-c#''-b'.

e. Arpeggiation from the first structural tone (this is the least likely, except in the later foreground—often turns out to be embellishment or merely a by-product of compound melody).

6. Register transfer is the most common cause of apparently confused upper-voice voice leading. Although the transfers may need to be retained in the foreground graph, an informal attempt should be made to correct some or all of them to locate the simpler, underlying patterns. Techniques closely related to—or depending on—register transfer are, of course, included in this, such as reaching-over, reaching-under, coupling, and boundary play. The last of these, usually prolongation of a cover tone, can be particularly troublesome since it raises doubts about the first note of the fundamental line. In some problematic cases, the first structural tone and a cover tone prolonged by boundary play can have almost equal significance, becoming effectively "dual" fundamental notes. Other than register transfer, the most common source of difficulty is a failure to recognize compound melody and trace the separate voice-leading strands.

Chapter 6: Middleground and Foreground Techniques

The middleground is the level, or series of levels, in which most of the refinement of voice-leading development occurs. Essential motives and characteristic chord progressions arise here and traditional form designs emerge. The foreground is not inherently different from the middleground(s): it is simply the last of this series of levels, the one with the most diminutions and, of course, the one closest to the score itself.

Schenker itemizes and discusses the specific features of the middleground in Part II, Chapter 2, of *Free Composition*. He concentrates on the first middleground; that is, the level immediately after the background containing the fundamental structure. The first middleground is the only level that contains what he calls "first-order" diminutions, or direct elaborations of individual tones of the fundamental structure. Chapter 2 of Part III (Foreground) is devoted to "the later structural levels," which in most instances includes both foreground and the later middleground. Be aware of this seeming discrepancy when you use *Free Composition* as a reference—which you should do often. Both chapters mentioned above have clearly marked subdivisions, each of which is given over to one of the topics explained and discussed below and includes multiple references to analyses in the Supplement volume. The translations of terms and abbreviations we employ here follow *Free Composition* as much as possible.

Two additional sources: 1) Cube, *The Book of the Musical Artwork*, Part II, §2 (pp. 205 ff.). This is an itemized list of techniques with brief explanations and many references to examples in analyses later in the book. 2) Jonas, *Introduction to the Theory of Heinrich Schenker*, Chapter 3. This chapter does not include all the techniques discussed below, but it has good examples and is particularly thorough on linear progressions. Explanations in Forte and Gilbert, *Introduction to Schenkerian Analysis*, are, unfortu-

nately, spread all about the book, though most are concentrated in Part II and the first two chapters of Part III. Similarly, the organization of the text and some differences in translation of terms in Salzer's *Structural Hearing* sometimes make it difficult to refer to material on individual voice-leading techniques.

INITIAL ASCENT (*ANSTIEG*) AND RISING LINES IN THE LATER LEVELS

The initial ascent (abbreviated "in.asc.") is a prefix to the first tone of the fundamental line. Strictly speaking it is a line based on an interval of the tonic triad, but for practical purposes we may regard it as a line, arpeggio, or combination of both. Instances of each might be $\hat{1}$-$\hat{2}$-$\hat{3}$, $\hat{5}$-$\hat{1}$-$\hat{3}$, or $\hat{5}$-$\hat{1}$-$\hat{2}$-$\hat{3}$, respectively, where $\hat{3}$ is the first note of the fundamental line. It is preferred, but not required, that each tone be separately harmonized. The initial ascent almost always results in displacement of the first soprano and bass note-pair in the fundamental structure (the background bass tonic supports the initial ascent, but the first tone of the fundamental line, of course, does not appear until the pattern is completed).

The simplest initial ascent is an unharmonized rising line, as illustrated in Ex. 6.1: the opening of the Pastoral Symphony from

EXAMPLE 6.1 Handel, *Messiah*, Pastoral Symphony, opening

Handel's *Messiah*. The Beethoven, Bagatelle, op. 119, no. 9, on the other hand, uses only triad tones (Ex. 6.2)—note that the first tone of the fundamental line is displaced by two bars, or half of the first phrase. In Exs. 6.3 and 6.4, arpeggiation and line are combined, though in both cases, the arpeggiation is clearly the overriding feature. In Ex. 6.5 (Mozart, Violin Sonata, K. 6, Menuet), the first structural tone is delayed until the end of the phrase, and the initial ascent is embellished by chromatic passing tones. Diminution of the tones of the initial ascent with notes or figures of later levels is a very common technique.

EXAMPLE 6.2 Beethoven, Bagatelle, op. 119, no. 9

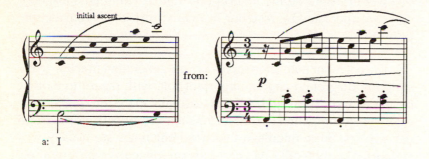

EXAMPLE 6.3 Haydn, Menuet in C Major

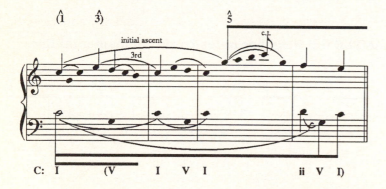

EXAMPLE 6.4 Chopin, Prelude in B Minor

EXAMPLE 6.5 Mozart, Violin Sonata, K. 6, Menuet

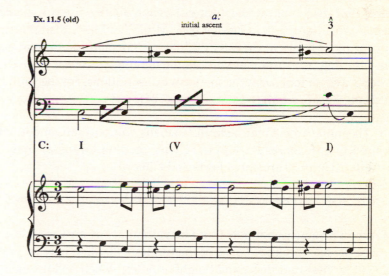

Generally, the displacement caused by the initial ascent does not affect the relationship between the fundamental structure and formal design, since the ascent is usually completed within the bounds of the first tonic-controlled form division (a phrase for a short piece, perhaps a period or more for a larger composition). But there are exceptions. See, for example Schenker's reading of the first movement of Beethoven's "Moonlight" Sonata (*Free Composition*, Fig. 7a) or the theme of the second movement of the "Appassionata" Sonata (Fig. 40,8; also in Forte and Gilbert, p. 155). It is also possible for the underlying harmony to change from the tonic to some other chord at the point the first note of the fundamental line is reached, as several of the examples in Figures 39 and 40 of *Free Composition* demonstrate (see, for instance, Fig. 40,10).

The initial ascent is the only rising line allowed the principal upper voice in the first middleground. In the second middleground or later one may also find a line from an established inner voice upward to a note of the fundamental line (see *Free Composition*, Figures 42,1 (Chopin) and 42,2 (Haydn)). Such lines are referred to as "motion from an inner voice" (mtn.inr.vc.). They are more likely to occur in developmental or transitional areas, as in the two figures just cited (but also look at the topmost graph in the Haydn sonata development analysis in *Five Graphic Music Analyses*). Rising lines appear more freely in the later middlegrounds and foreground, as lines leading from an inner voice to the main upper voice, from the latter to a cover tone, or as the smallest of diminutions. For the "initial descent" figure, see the section "Lines" below.

The initial ascent may be found in many compositions and is not limited to any genre. As supplementary reading on initial ascent, consult Chapters 9 and 10 of Forte and Gilbert.

NEIGHBOR NOTES TO TONES OF THE FUNDAMENTAL LINE

Motion with a neighbor note (n.n.) may occur at any structural level except the background. Tones of the fundamental line may be prolonged by first-middleground neighbor notes, which will normally also acquire consonant harmonic support. These are associated with a substantial key region, major formal division, or a strategic dramatic or formal point in the composition. Neighbor notes may be either diatonic or chromatic and in all but a very few cases are *above* the structural tone. The most common are $\hat{4}$ embellishing $\hat{3}$ or $\hat{6}$ embellishing $\hat{5}$ (see Ex. 6.6). The non-tonic triad notes in the fundamental line ($\hat{4}$, $\hat{2}$; or $\hat{7}$, $\hat{6}$ in the 8-line) are not so often prolonged by neighbor notes.

The repeated tone is the simplest of all prolongations; complete neighbor-note motions are diminutions of this repetition. Incomplete neighbor motions, the escape tone and appoggiatura, are specialized variants. Only lines, the other class of step-wise patterns, will occur so often as neighbor notes at all levels. The escape-tone figure $\hat{3}$-$\hat{4}$-$\hat{2}$-$\hat{1}$ may occur in earlier levels of structure, especially when the $\hat{4}$ is associated with a IV or ii in the cadence that brings the fundamental line to a close. The appoggiatura may belong to the second middleground when it acts as a prefix to the first note of the fundamental line, thus "replacing" an initial ascent. Otherwise, the incomplete figures, whether escape tones or appoggiaturas, are generally foreground phenomena.

Schenker specifically forbids the diatonic lower neighbor to $\hat{3}$, since this would duplicate the interruption figure. Chromatic neighbor notes are understood as resulting from mixture (see "Chromaticism" below).

The neighbor note often serves a form-generating function in the early middleground and an important role with regard to motivic design, as well. The neighbor note is essential to the interpretation of extended or compound ternary forms such as rondos (rondeaux) and dance pairs. Since middleground neighbor notes are usually well supported harmonically, they are easily prolonged. A typical example of a middleground neighbor note and mixture in a small dance form is the first of Schubert's *Wiener-Damen Walzer*, D.734 (Ex. 6.7; score in Ex. 1.14). The neighbor note $\hat{6}$ generates section B1 and its harmoni-

EXAMPLE 6.6 Neighbor notes to the fundamental line

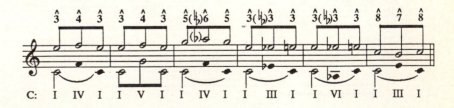

zation with VI, which is prolonged as a key region, creates mixture. Note that the effect is emphasized by the lack of a returning modulatory progression.

EXAMPLE 6.7 Schubert, Wiener-Damen Walzer, D. 734, no. 1

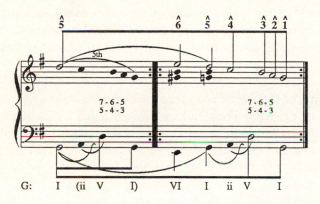

Do not overlook the potential for even the smallest details of the latest levels to provide clues to hearing structural features. The anacrusis and bar 1 of this waltz offer three possible tonic-chord tones to begin the fundamental line. Of these three, the d″ is not the strongest candidate, because it acts as a pick-up note. In bar 2 the situation changes. We readily hear d″ as an appoggiatura to c″ (4–3 over the bass A), the eighth-rest notwithstanding. Thus, it is apparent that c″ is part of a foreground line that descends from d″ (d″-c″-b′-a′-(g′ implied)) in bars 1–4, not a neighbor note to the b′ in bar 1. Note that d″ in bar 2 can be understood as part of the underlying V⁷ harmony. Here, however, its *melodic* or *contrapuntal* role is clearly more significant. The motion e″-d″ in bar 4 confirms our hearing of this passage with another appoggiatura figure, this time embellishing the repetition of the structural note, $\hat{5}$. Finally, in bar 6 the d″ becomes a simple non-chord-tone appoggiatura above ii. If the d″-c″ figures are clues to the principal upper voice at the beginning, the e″-d″ in bar 4 points toward larger-scale structures, since the complete neighbor figure d″-e″-d″ is the upper-voice motion in the first middleground for bars 1–17. One last detail: As e″ ($\hat{6}$) is prolonged in bars 9–16, the

only surface figures used are repeated notes, simple chord arpeggiations, and neighbor notes (as in bars 11 or 15).

Also, see *Free Composition*, Fig. 35,1 (Mozart, Sonata, K. 331, II); 40,1 (Chopin, Polonaise, op. 40, no. 1); 42, 1 (Chopin, Etude, op. 10, no. 2); 42, 2 (Haydn, St. Anthony Chorale); 76,5 (Chopin, Mazurka, op. 17, no. 1); 153,1 (Chopin, Ballade, op. 23); and 153,2 (Chopin, Etude, op. 10, no. 3). Figures 76–80 give a series of examples of neighbor notes.

MIXTURE (*MISCHUNG*)

Strictly speaking, the fundamental structure may contain no chromaticism of any kind. A background graph that includes inner voices may have chromatic tones, such as the leading tone in the minor key, in one of those voices, but not in the fundamental line or bass arpeggiation. The first middleground may contain neighbor notes, inflections arising from mixture, and leading tones. Later levels are increasingly more free in their treatment of chromatic elements.

Thus, fundamental lines notated to include chromatic tones are actually fundamental lines *plus* one or more middleground elements, just as fundamental lines with interruption include a middleground element. Such "chromatic fundamental lines" include 1) a line from $\hat{3}$ in which the mode changes, as, for instance, occurs in Schubert Lieder; see the model in the second part of Ex. 6.8a; 2) a line from $\hat{3}$ with an inflection or chromatic neighbor note arising from mixture, such as Major: $\natural\hat{3}$-$\flat\hat{3}$-$\natural\hat{3}$; see Ex. 6.6 or *Free Composition*, Fig. 30,a (Chopin); or 3) a line with a chromatic passing tone, such as Major: $\natural\hat{3}$-$\flat\hat{3}$-$\hat{2}$-$\hat{1}$ or $\hat{8}$-$\hat{7}$-$\flat\hat{7}$-$\hat{6}$-$\hat{5}$-$\hat{4}$-$\hat{3}$-$\hat{2}$-$\hat{1}$; see the second and fourth models in Ex. 6.8b.

Chromaticism is interpreted in Schenkerian theory exclusively as elaboration of a diatonic model; that is, chromatic tones are understood to be altered diatonic tones. This corresponds for the most part with traditional views: for instance, the $\flat\hat{2}$ in the Neapolitan chord is understood as an altered $\natural\hat{2}$; the chromatic mediant degrees are altered diatonic mediants; and so on. In the reduction phase of work on an analysis, try to reduce a chromatic feature to the underlying diatonic model or else "contain" it as prolongation of some deeper-level diatonic feature. The analysis of Bach, C-Major Prelude, in *Five*

Graphic Music Analyses provides an instance of each of these: 1) bar 23 of the score foreground contains a ii$^{\varnothing6}_5$ harmony; this is shown as ii$^6_5$ in the middleground; 2) chromatic tones in bars 1-19 are all understood as part of the foreground prolongation of the register transfer (coupling) of e'' to e'. In cases where the chromatic feature substitutes for a diatonic one which does not appear at all, implied tones or sonorities must sometimes be used. This is most likely to happen in later nineteenth-century music.

EXAMPLE 6.8a First-middleground forms generated by mixture, applied to baroque dance pair (1) or 19th-century Lied (2)

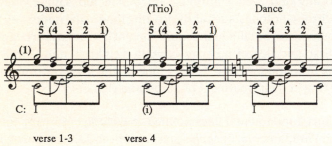

EXAMPLE 6.8b Some first-middleground forms generated by mixture

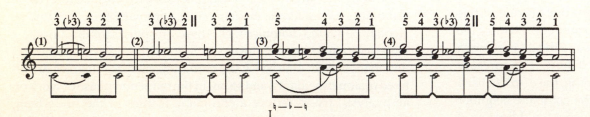

The source of chromaticism in the early middleground—and an important source later on, too—is mixture, a term which refers to the nineteenth-century notion of "mixing" two tonalities or scale forms, so that tones or sonorities from one may be used in the other. The notion of "borrowing" or "borrowed chords" often presented in harmony textbooks is derived from this. The topic may be divided into three points: 1) mode change (parallel major and minor); 2) chromatic mediant harmonic progressions; 3) $\flat\hat{2}$, which Schenker calls the "Phrygian $\hat{2}$" and which applies mainly to the familiar Neapolitan chord.

Some of the forms produced by direct mode change are illustrated in Ex. 6.8b. Those which return to the original mode are applicable to Baroque dance pairs and similar pieces: see the first part of Ex. 6.8a. In *Free Composition*, examine Figs. 40,6 (Beethoven, Sonata, op. 26, III) and 155,4 (Mozart, Rondo, K. 511).

The chromatic mediant progression produces a variety of patterns, some of which produce changes only in inner parts, not in the fundamental line. Change of bass (as in I-$\flat$III) below $\hat{5}$ or the harmonization of a chromatic neighbor note may be sources of chromatic mediants. In addition to Ex. 6.7 above, we cite Schenker's Fig. 30,a (Chopin, Mazurka, op. 17, no.3) with $\natural$3-$\flat$3-$\natural$3 above I-$\flat$VI-I.

The Phrygian $\hat{2}$ or $\flat\hat{2}$ is used in reference to the Neapolitan Sixth (N^6), which is understood as an altered ii$^{\circ6}$—therefore, the $\flat\hat{2}$ is derived from $\natural\hat{2}$. Since the $\flat\hat{2}$ normally moves downward to $\hat{1}$ and $\hat{7}$, the $\natural\hat{2}$ must be added in parentheses: $\flat\hat{2}$ ($\natural\hat{2}$)-$\hat{1}$-$\hat{7}$. In Ex. 6.9, the $\flat\hat{2}$ is involved in an interruption as well as in the final descent of the fundamental line. The notation is similar. Schenker illustrates the $\flat\hat{2}$ in *Free Composition*, Figure 31.

As additional reading on mixture, consult *Structural Hearing*, pp. 177-81.

EXAMPLE 6.9 Beethoven, Bagatelle, op. 119, no. 9

CHROMATICISM AT LATER LEVELS

Most examples in this book have involved chromaticism in some fashion. Bach's setting of the chorale "Du Friedensfürst" (Chapter 5) contains only one chromatic note, which adorns the foreground in an inner voice, creating a leading tone (E♯) for a tonicization of vi. The Invention in G Major, likewise, has very few chromatic tones, but some play more structurally significant roles. The second-order sixth-line prolonging g″ (8̂) at the beginning includes f♯″, which effectively identifies the line as a later feature of the composing-out; that is, f♯″ is *not* the 7̂ of the fundamental line (see Ex. 5.12). The f♯″ inflection also returns in bar 17 as part of the boundary play above d″. The only other chromatic tone is C♯, stated several times as the leading tone in the tonicization of D major in bars 7-14. One of these

statements is part of the leading-tone third-line e″-d″-c♯″ in the cadence of bars 12-13, and the note has been retained as an inner voice in the background graph.

At the opposite extreme, Bach's setting of "Christ lag in Todesbanden" as the last movement of Cantata No. 4 (Ex. 6.10) presents a complex but tightly controlled chromatic surface which organizes its chromaticism in a series of local key regions. The second note of the melody, a♯′, forces surprisingly quick motion into a dominant key region, the return to the tonic region being affected by means of V♮-♯ (that is, the third of the dominant changes from minor to major, one of the most common chromatic techniques in minor key

EXAMPLE 6.10 J. S. Bach, setting of "Christ lag in Todesbanden"

compositions). Bach uses the same ♮-♯ device again in bar 7, now with the tonic, but the interplay of the two tones involved in bars 1-2, that is, D-natural and D-sharp, becomes motivic (alto, bar 3, bars 5 and 6; soprano, bars 7-8; alto against bass, bar 11). In bar 7, d♯''', like the a♯' in bar 1, "announces" the progression that immediately follows on a chromatic ascending line in the bass. The unstable harmonic successions in bars 7-10 rest on a triadic bass arpeggiation (shown in a separate staff underneath—small e-great B-G-E), which is itself followed by another bass arpeggiation (bars 10-11).

Thus, the underlying (middleground) patterning of the bass is diatonic, and Bach makes use of the rather free arpeggiations involving i, III, and v (or V) that are typical features of minor-key compositions as strong structural determinants for his setting.

LINES (ZUG; PLURAL ZÜGE)

Lines are the most common of all melodic phenomena at every level. With rare exceptions, lines must fill consonant intervals, and those intervals should be capable of interpretation as the composing-out of intervals in underlying harmonies (with allowance for functional substitution). In other words, in almost all cases the interval spanned by a linear progression will be a component of a harmonic function relevant to the context. The interpretation of underlying intervals in lines in the bass, on the other hand, may be freer, since these lines are often filling in a harmonic step (that is, motion between chord roots). Normally, the first pitch of a descending line is the one that belongs to the next deeper level, but the last pitch of an ascending line belongs to the next deeper level. Thus, a descending line signifies motion from an upper voice to an inner voice, but an ascending line signifies motion from an inner voice to an upper voice.

Lines in the middleground often function as the main structural feature of the upper part in form sections. Because the linear progression finds its original model in the fundamental line, it happens frequently that a specific linear progression in a subsequent level reflects the form of the fundamental line. This follows Schenker's idea of "repetition," which is the basis of "concealed repetition," a topic discussed at length in Chapter 7. (Next to lines, neighbor notes are most susceptible to this process.)

The treatment of the different classes of lines varies depending on the context, position in upper voice or bass, type of harmonic support, and so on, but we can make a few general comments, nevertheless.

The third-line (3-line) is certainly the most common of all. These lines fill the thirds in underlying chords, frequently appearing in the foreground as offshoots from a main tone into an inner voice, or "inner-third-lines" (*Innenterzzüge*: inr.3-line). In foreground and middleground, a special type of inner-third-line moves from $\hat{2}$ downward to $\hat{7}$, often in cadential situations. The Invention in G Major makes use of this leading-tone third-line (*Leitton-Terzzug*: l.t.3-line) in the cadence to the dominant, bars 12-13, and also in the closing cadence. The standard resolution of the ♭$\hat{2}$ in the Neapolitan chord—♭$\hat{2}$ (♮$\hat{2}$)-$\hat{1}$-$\hat{7}$—is a chromatic variant of the leading-tone third-line.

Fifth-lines also appear frequently and, in descending form, are often used for longer spans of music with prolongation of the individual elements, as, for instance, the main upper-voice pattern in a tonally closed form section (see Ex. 6.7, bars 1-8). The second-order fifth-line from $\hat{2}$ is another example (most extended forms with interruption make use of this, including the sonata). Rising fifth-lines appear in the bass covering the interval from $\hat{1}$ to $\hat{5}$, the fifth usually being subdivided into two thirds or a third and the functional progression IV-V or ii⁶-V. (Also see *Free Composition*, pp. 76-77; Fig. 88.)

Fourth-lines are typically found where the upper voice starts on the fifth scale degree and descends to the second in conjunction with harmonic motion from I to V. This is one of the few instances where an upper-voice line does not have the support of a single harmony. In the bass, the fourth-line acts like an inverted fifth—that is, it covers the distance from $\hat{5}$ to $\hat{8}$—but it can also move from $\hat{1}$ (or $\hat{8}$) downward to $\hat{5}$. The same motions in the upper voices are normally foreground details, though an "initial descent" is possible. This is a special type of unsupported stretch (*Leerlauf*), that is, a linear motion from a superimposed inner voice or cover tone downward to the first note of the fundamental line. The "initial descent" is not a frequent occurrence and normally involves a line from $\hat{8}$ down to $\hat{5}$, or rarely a line from $\hat{8}$ down to $\hat{3}$—see the discussion and example in Forte and Gilbert, pp. 181-183. (Also see *Free Composition*, p. 76; Fig. 87.)

Lines of the diminished fifth or augmented fourth are possible in the foreground, but are often better interpreted as incidental lines within the unfolding of an interval in a dominant seventh or diminished seventh chord.

Sixth-lines are more likely in the later levels and may often be better interpreted as "filled-in" unfoldings (that is, the unfolded interval of the sixth takes priority over the line that leads through it). The sixth-line in the opening bars of our analysis of the Invention in G Major might have been treated this way (as incidental to an unfolded g''-b'), but we decided that, in this case, the linear progression, which belongs to the middleground, was more significant. (Also see *Free Composition*, p. 77; Fig. 89.)

Lines of the seventh or ninth are not true lines; they are composed-out steps to which register transfer has been applied. They are frequently divided into thirds and are often found in sequence constructions. The most likely line of the seventh is one that spans the distance from the root to the seventh of an underlying seventh chord, such as V^7 or ii^7. See *Five Graphic Music Analyses*, Haydn Sonata development (also in *Free Composition*, Fig. 62,1). (Also see *Free Composition*, p. 77; Figs. 62,1-4.)

The line of the octave is usually best understood as an embellishment of a register transfer. An octave-line may also be subdivided, usually into a fifth and a fourth ($\hat{1}$-$\hat{5}$, $\hat{5}$-$\hat{8}$, respectively), but occasionally into other intervals as well (fourth and two thirds; three thirds and a second). The section Register Transfer below has more information. (Also see *Free Composition*, p. 77; Fig. 90.)

As additional references, use Chapter 19 of Forte and Gilbert, particularly the cautionary section "dissonant and false linear pro-

gressions" (pp. 240-245); and Jonas, *Introduction*, Chapter 3,1-2. Also consult the discussion of the combination of lines in *Free Composition*, pp. 78-82.

INTERRUPTION *(UNTERBRECHUNG)*

Interruption is one of the most common features of the first middleground, but it may occur at any later level as well. The figure $\hat{3}$-$\hat{2}$ is understood as an interrupted third-line $\hat{3}$-$\hat{2}$-($\hat{1}$), and $\hat{5}$-$\hat{4}$-$\hat{3}$-$\hat{2}$ as an interrupted fifth-line $\hat{5}$-$\hat{4}$-$\hat{3}$-$\hat{2}$-($\hat{1}$). The second $\hat{3}$-$\hat{2}$ and the apparent fourth-line $\hat{5}$-$\hat{4}$-$\hat{3}$-$\hat{2}$ are acceptable under these circumstances, even though the interval outlined is not part of one underlying triad. The interruption is one of the most powerful delineators of formal design and, according to Schenker, is a requirement for the sonata.

The excerpt from Beethoven, Bagatelle, op. 119, no. 9 in Ex. 6.9 above is section A of a binary/ternary form. Thus, the interruption shown in the example is a second-middleground feature. (As it happens, section B prolongs V, creating a first-middleground interruption.) Under the section Boundary Play below is an analysis of Brahms, Intermezzo, op. 76, no. 7, a work which uses interruption as the main feature of a rounded binary design. For a typical example of the treatment of interruption in the sonata, see the discussion of Beethoven, Piano Sonata, op. 14, no. 2, I, in Chapter 8. Finally, a detail of notation: the two vertical lines which further identify the interruption should be placed immediately after the $\hat{2}$, not at the end of any prolongation of the $\hat{2}$ that might (and very often does) follow.

Also, see *Free Composition*, Figs. 7a (Beethoven, op. 27, no. 1, I); Fig. 12 (Chopin, Etude, op. 10, no. 12)—also in *Five Graphic Music Analyses* ; 22b (Schumann "Aus meinen Thränen spriessen"); 35,1 (Mozart, K. 331, II); and others.

REGISTER TRANSFER

In the most general sense, register transfer is displacement of any note in the voice leading by an octave, either up or down. The voice leading for the part involved may then continue in the new register or at some point return to the original, perhaps by way of a second register transfer. Register transfer may be used at any level of composing-out except the background and is accomplished by direct octave leap, by arpeggiation, by line, or by a combination of arpeggiation and line.

Several German terms are associated with this technique:

1. *Höherlegung,* translated in *Free Composition* as "ascending octave transfer" or "ascending register transfer," (asc.rg.tr.) refers simply to moving a note or voice up an octave.

2. *Tieferlegung,* "descending octave transfer" or "descending register transfer," (desc.rg.tr.) refers to moving a note or voice down an octave.

3. *Übergreifen* or "reaching-over," (rg.-ov.) refers specifically to an ascending register transfer of a figure of two or more notes in descending stepwise motion (such as F-E or B♭-A). The term also emphasizes the leap over another continuing voice (usually the principal upper voice). Often, reaching-over will occur two or three times in immediate succession. Instances of reaching-over, from Chopin mazurkas, are shown in Exs. 6.11a and b.[1] Forte and Gilbert call *Übergreifen* "overlapping."

4. *Untergreifen* , literally "reaching-under," includes not only motion from an upper voice into the inner voices, but also the correcting "motion from an inner voice" which returns to the correct upper register. "Motion from an inner voice" (mtn.inr.vc.) is the translation used in *Free Composition.*

---

[1] These examples, along with Ex. 6.13, are taken from Nicol Viljoen, "Motivic Design and Tonal Structure in the Mazurkas of Frederic Chopin," (Ph.D. dissertation, University of the OFS [South Africa], 1989), pp. 192, 172, respectively. © 1989 Nicolas Viljoen. Reprinted by permission.

EXAMPLE 6.11a Chopin, Mazurka, op. 6, No. 1, bars 1-2

EXAMPLE 6.11b Chopin, Mazurka. op. 50, No. 3, bars 37-41

5. *Koppelung*, or "coupling," is the middleground phenomenon of linear "doubling" of a tone or tones of the fundamental line. For example, where the latter is e''-d''-c'', coupling may produce a figure e''-(e'-d')-d''-c''—as in the C Major Prelude from the Well-Tempered Clavier (see Chapter 5 above).

Register transfer in its various guises may be applied to any note of the fundamental line, but it is a more common technique in the later levels. Early in a composition, a change of register upward from the first note of the line often indicates initial ascent. Also, register transfer applied to î typically belongs to the foreground or the later middleground. Reaching-over belongs to the foreground, but it may also function as a middleground device when it is involved in initial ascent patterns.

On the other hand, middleground coupling of registers is not infrequent, especially if a note of the fundamental line is involved. Once registral relations have been established by the couplings, it is possible to refer to these in subtle and artistic ways and to develop progressions which incorporate register in a structural (even motivic) fashion, not merely as a decorative factor (or simple diminution).

No register transfers, including couplings, may be part of the background. There, following the rules of strict counterpoint, the fundamental line must move within a single octave: this is the rule of obligatory register (*obligate Lage*). If the fundamental line actually closes in a different register than it began, it must be assumed that a register transfer or coupling has occurred in the first middleground and this must be "corrected" in the background (as in Ex. 6.12). The register chosen is usually—but not necessarily—that of the final descent of the fundamental line, or the î.

Also, see *Free Composition*, Figs. 41, 42, 101, 102 (several examples in each figure). The discussions of coupling in Forte and Gilbert are concise and clear (pp. 167-169, 260-264), as is their first discussion of overlapping (p. 221).

EXAMPLE 6.12 Correction of register for obligatory register

ARPEGGIATION

Arpeggiation (arpeg. or arp.) is one of the most direct ways to prolong or unfold an underlying harmony. A figure may be generated in any voice by arpeggiation of a supporting harmony, and arpeggiations frequently coincide with passing melodic motions filling in some or all of the spaces of the chord intervals. In the latter case, the linear elements are subordinate to the arpeggiated harmony; thus, at a deeper level one must decide if the unfolded chord is the true figure or whether it should be collapsed into a vertical, as shown in Ex. 6.13. In general, give preference to lines over arpeggiations where the choice arises, except in the smallest and last diminutions. Remember, though, that this is by no means a hard-and-fast rule.

In the middleground, arpeggiation is employed in particular in connection with elaboration of the fundamental bass motion from I to

EXAMPLE 6.13 Chopin, Mazurka. op. 59, No. 1, bars 1-4, melody only

EXAMPLE 6.14 C. P. E. Bach, Sonatas, Rondos, and Fantasies, vol. 4, Rondo in A, bars 1-4

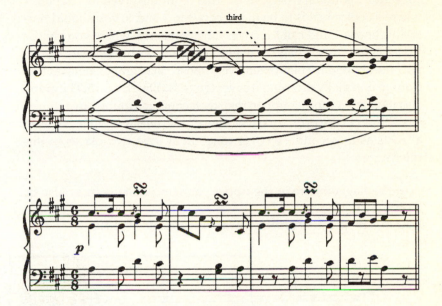

V, or I-III-V (i-III-V in the minor), with the initial ascent, and as a subsidiary part of a coupling figure. The first of these especially can have consequences for form design.

An interesting nesting of elaborated foreground arpeggiations occurs in the opening bars of a C. P. E. Bach Rondo (Ex. 6.14). The overall progression of the upper voice is a third-line (an enlargement of the third-line in bar 1); the first two bars are governed by a descending arpeggiation which also accomplishes a register transfer of 3̂ (c#″ to c#′). The first interval, c#″-a′, is filled in with the third-line, as is the last interval, e′-c#′, but the fourth a′-e′ is prolonged by a direct arpeggiation (which creates a brief cover tone e″ and, in its own way, is a reflection of the larger arpeggiation through the octave). All in all, this is a remarkably tightly built motivic and voice-leading structure which, nevertheless, has the simplicity and melodiousness an eighteenth-century listener would have expected of a rondo theme.

BOUNDARY PLAY (*RÄNDERSPIEL*) AND COVER TONE (*DECKTON*)

Activity above the primary or structural voice is referred to as boundary play (Forte and Gilbert use "covering progression" [224]). If one tone used in boundary play is emphasized or isolated, it is called a cover tone. More often than not, the cover tone will belong to the tonic triad, but this is not a requirement. Schenker himself says of the cover tone that "it constantly attracts the attention of the ear, even though the essential voice-leading events take place beneath it" (*Free Composition*, p. 107). Boundary play is used only in later middlegrounds and the foreground; in working out an analysis, it is often easiest to regard it as the elaboration, or even prolongation, of a cover tone. The symbol used for the cover tone is a stemmed closed note with "c.t." or a flagged note with or without "c.t." Boundary play may be identified by "b.p." or "b. play."

A prominent cover tone can be the source of uncertainty about the first tone of the fundamental line, particularly if it is part of substantial boundary play. In the rule of thumb given in Chapter 5, where a choice needs to be made between 3̂ and 5̂, you should normally choose 3̂ and call 5̂ a cover tone. Similarly, where you choose 5̂ over 8̂, the latter will be a cover tone. Brahms's Intermezzo, op. 76, no. 7 uses boundary play extensively, most of it neighbor-note motion from an unusually prominent cover tone e'' (5̂). See Ex. 6.15. The graph also illustrates another upper-register technique: double cover tones. In addition to the primary cover tone e'', the next triad tone above it, a'', acts as a "secondary cover tone" in at least two places in this Intermezzo.

The flagged note in the upper parts, incidentally, may also be used to identify "interesting notes"; that is, foreground notes to which you want to draw attention for some reason (because of an unusual chromaticism, reference to a significant register, or other feature) but which are not otherwise significant in the main voice-leading progressions. This flagging of such notes is related to the exclamation point (!) which Schenker uses to draw attention to some unexpected feature of the voice-leading fabric or harmony (as in *Five Graphic Music Analyses*, Chopin, F Major Etude, *Urlinie-Tafel*, bar 76). If you identify "interesting notes" in a graph, then use the stemmed note with "c.t." to identify cover tones.

See *Free Composition*, Fig. 75 (a complex collection of cover tones in a Chopin mazurka). Forte and Gilbert discuss the cover tone on pp. 223-228.

EXAMPLE 6.15 Brahms, Intermezzo, op. 76, no. 7

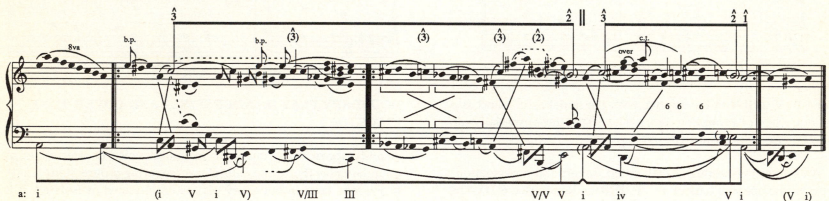

VOICE EXCHANGE (*STIMMTAUSCH*)

Voice exchange is a derivative of arpeggiation or simple chordal unfolding. In Ex. 6.16a-c, the most common form is illustrated: 10-6 or 6-10. The less common 5-4 (or 4-5) and dim.5-aug.4 (or aug.4-dim.5) appear in Exs. 6.16d-e. The exchange must occur within a single harmony, though there may, of course, be intermediate embellishing chords. Exceptions are made for harmonies which are functionally identical and related at the third, such as V and vii° or I and vi.

Chromatic changes may also be applied, as in Ex. 6.16f, where the functional relationship is more complex: both iv⁶ and vii°/V *lead to* V).

Like the register transfer, voice exchange may be a simple prolonging device without effect on the voice leading or it may join or connect with continuing voices. Voice exchange occurs mainly in the foreground. Brahms's op. 76, no. 7 (Ex. 6.15) includes several instances of voice exchange.

Also consult Forte and Gilbert, pp. 110-119.

EXAMPLE 6.16 Voice exchange

UNFOLDING (*AUSFALTUNG*)

Unfolding (unf.), which was discussed in connection with the bass in Chapter 1, may be described as a special case of composing-out by arpeggiation. In the upper parts, unfolded intervals most often come in pairs (or longer series) and are most often thirds or sixths. The pair dim.5-3 or aug.4-6 is also possible.

Because there is some ambiguity in Schenker's treatment of unfolding (*Free Composition*, p. 50), it is often difficult to know when to apply its special symbol in the upper parts.[2] Normally, use it in the following circumstances:

1. For pairs of thirds in the foreground;

2. For dim.5-3 or aug.4-6 in foreground or middleground;

3. For the diminished fifth or augmented fourth in isolation (to avoid notating a line of the tritone, for instance, or to emphasize

---

[2]This is also an instance where differences in notational style come into play: Cube made a much closer link between unfolding and arpeggiation than did other Schenker students, and thus his graphs often show unusually large numbers of unfoldings. See his graphs of Bach Inventions reproduced in the Exercises for Part II below.

the interval rather than the line);

4. Rarely, for parallel diminished fifths or augmented fourths;

5. For the isolated composed-out interval (most often the sixth, occasionally the tritone, not the octave) where there is no complete or correct line. Instead of an octave unfolding, use register transfer.

The technique of unfolding belongs to all the levels (except the background), but is most common in the foreground. Unfoldings may sometimes be presented on a larger scale, controlling many foreground diminutions, as well as problematic foreground passages in which underlying harmonic/voice-leading derivations are difficult to assess, due to complicated surface chromatic motions and the like. Some instances of unfolding in Brahms's op. 76, no. 7 are shown in Ex. 6.15. Also, see the analysis of Bach's G-Major Invention in Chapter 5—especially the foreground.

Finally, we repeat a point about notation from Chapter 1: Always write the unfolding symbol so that the stems of the notes point "inward"; that is, toward the center of the interval being unfolded. This makes a much more compact, better-looking symbol than pointing the stems "outward" or away from the interval.

For additional examples, see *Free Composition*, Figs. 46,2 (Schubert); 47 (Mozart); 103 (several examples). Also consult Forte and Gilbert, pp. 251-60.

[EXERCISES II.1-II.17.]
A preliminary reading of this chapter may be followed by assignments linked with closer reading of sections discussing the pertinent techniques.

Chapter 7: Essay on Chopin, Prelude in A♭ Major, op. 28, no. 17

The following expands on the narratives of Chapters 2 and 5 to provide a sample of a complete essay based on a Schenkerian analysis. The particular issue explored here is the role of motivic design in tonal structure.

If we can understand the structural bass arpeggiation, the I-V-I, as the essence of harmony, we can also grasp motive (or motivic germ) and line as the twin essences of melody, and strict counterpoint as the essence of the combination of melody and harmony. Seen from the standpoint of composing-out, the fundamental structure thus acts as the original "cell" of harmony, line, and counterpoint. This cell is integrated with motivic development in the structures of the first and second middleground, where motives arise which can be repeated or elaborated in the later levels of composing-out, including the most immediate figures of the score itself. Seen from the reductive standpoint, surface motives can also appear at deeper levels, a phenomenon Schenker calls "concealed repetition."

The recurrence of motives at the various structural levels was very important to Schenker; in fact, at times he seemed to regard it as a means of structuring melody nearly equal in importance to the fundamental line. Instead of the common nineteenth-century understanding of melody, which was essentially narrative, with its thematic development and leading motives, Schenker wanted melody to be another element in the complex but organically unified musical system of each composition. Master composers, in other words, were understood to "improvise" motivic connections between the levels in the course of composing-out from the background.

As an example of this masterly improvisation, we can examine the Prelude in A♭ from Chopin's Preludes, op. 28. This work has the character and expression of a ballade in miniature, and—perhaps in part because the ballade was one of the most serious and poetic of his large forms—it is not surprising that Chopin seems to have devoted special attention to making this a closely integrated and rich work,

despite its small compass. The murmuring chords of the opening (even including the placement of the hands!) and the first sweep of melody in bars 3-4 present all the essential motivic material from which the Prelude evolves. The treatment of these motives has consequences not just in melodic patterning, but in harmony and the tonal design as well.

Despite its brevity, the Prelude clearly conveys the design of a five-part rondo (the complete score appears in Ex. 7.1). The theme is a period 18 bars long (2 + 16), and consists of two eight-bar phrase-pairs with an antecedent-consequent relationship; in other words, the theme has the regularity and simplicity generally expected of a rondo theme:

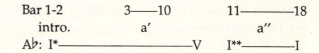

Here, "I*" refers to the fact that the tonic chord is presented in $^6_4$ position, which might lead one to hear the opening bars as V^6_4—$^5_3$. But Chopin never treats the chord unambiguously as the "cadential dominant" and so we may reasonably take it as a tonic representative at the opening. The label "I**" indicates that the tonic is not stated as a triad in bar 12, but, as in bars 3-4, is altered to V^7/IV. As we shall see, this ambiguity in the tonic chord at the opening—like other traits of the harmony—has unexpected consequences later in the composition.

The first digression encompasses bars 19-34. Its orienting point is a cadence to E Major (enharmonic for F♭ Major, or ♭VI) in bars 26-27. A brief transition (bars 32-34) leads to a return of the antecedent phrase-pair, now in a dramatic *fortissimo*. The second digression immediately follows (bars 43-64), leading first to E Major (= ♭VI) again, then F♯ Major (= ♭VII?), but eventually cadencing securely on E♭ Major (or V) in bar 57. This dominant is prolonged with a pedal point till a full reprise of the rondo theme begins in bar 65. This reprise, which includes almost all the original material but now set above a tonic pedal point, would close in bar 80, but the melodic line is extended to close in bar 84. A coda based on the second-inversion tonic chord of the introduction follows (bars 84-90). The entire plan may be represented as follows:

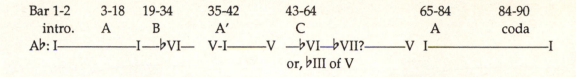

Bar 1-2	3-18	19-34	35-42	43-64	65-84	84-90
intro.	A	B	A'	C	A	coda

Ab: I————————I —bVI— V-I————V —bVI—bVII?————V I————————I
                                    or, bIII of V

The design of this framework is not unusual, but the composer animates it in a strikingly effective way. The placement of the tone c' in the right hand, literally under the left hand's eb', though apparently a small thing, has two immediate consequences that echo throughout the life of this composition. First, it shows in the most concrete possible fashion the structural relationship of c' and eb': c' is 3̂, the primary melodic tone (that is, first tone of the fundamental line); eb' is 5̂, which acts as a cover tone, but one important enough to generate much of the content of the two digressions. This arrangement of tonal space in itself forms an essential motive in this Prelude. Second, the placement of c' will make it clear in performance that the upper-voice melodic motion from bar 2 to bar 3 is c'-db', not eb'-db'. The neighbor-note figure c'-db'-c' (3̂-4̂-3̂) and others derived from it constitute the second essential motive. See Ex. 7.2.

A final motivic element that is perhaps a minor feature of the theme but which is exploited particularly in the digressions—chromaticism—arises in bar 4 with gb', which produces V^7/IV. The gb' is best understood as a chromatic passing tone which forces the leading tone g' (bar 3) downward to f' (bar 5). In any case, it reflects a characteristic feature of the rondo theme that links it closely with the digressions; that is, motivic development affects both harmonic and melodic dimensions. See Ex. 7.3.

The interplay of harmony and motive is particularly strong in the theme. In bar 5, for example, the subdominant harmony is plainly tied to the neighbor note: c' in bar 4 moves to db' (bar 5, left hand), which is prolonged until bar 8, where it resolves to c'. (This motion in the octave from c' may be assumed to double an implied, identical figure

EXAMPLE 7.2 Bars 1-3, beat 1

The third and fourth bars present the first sub-phrase of the rondo theme as well as the remaining motives. The quick move from db' to db'' in bar 3 generates a motive that will be used in two ways: first, two distinct structural registers are established, about the fourth and fifth octaves, respectively, or c' and eb' and c'' and eb''. Second, the idea of octave change or register transfer is established, an essential melodic feature of the two digressions.

EXAMPLE 7.3 Bars 3-5

EXAMPLE 7.1 Chopin, Preludes, op. 28, no. 17 in A♭, score

EXAMPLE 7.1 continued

EXAMPLE 7.1 continued

EXAMPLE 7.1 continued

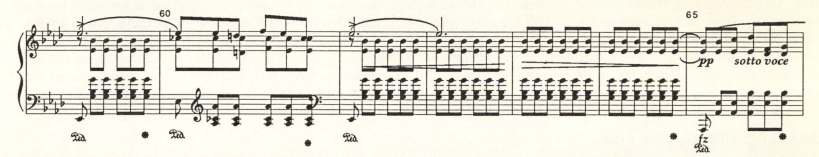

in the octave from c″, the obligatory register of the fundamental line.) From this subdominant chord in bar 5 arise two important transformations of earlier motives: The cover tone $\hat{5}$ acquires a neighbor note ($\hat{5}$-$\hat{6}$-$\hat{5}$), which is responsible for the striking and beautiful retrogression V⁷-IV-V⁷ (eb″-f″-eb″ in the soprano); and the octave change of bar 3 is transposed to ab′-ab″, which, enharmonically as g#′-g#″, is the principal melodic motion of the first digression.

In bar 8, the roles of the tones are reversed as c″ becomes a neighbor to db″. Once again a leading tone, here, a♮′, is forced downward (to ab′, and eventually to g′ in bar 10). In bar 9, the left-hand thumb brings $\hat{6}$ down to $\hat{5}$ in the fourth octave just before the right hand brings $\hat{4}$ down to $\hat{3}$ in the fifth octave. Both have the sound of appoggiatura figures (deriving from bb′-ab′ in bar 4), but they are more than lovely surface details: they are middleground-level resolutions of the neighbor notes introduced in bar 5. See Ex. 7.4, a detailed graph of the entire rondo theme.

EXAMPLE 7.4 Theme (bars 1-18)

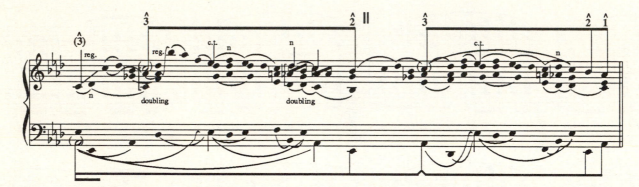

The first digression is based on the register (or octave) motive, neighbor notes, and, in the foreground, chromatic passing tones. The essential middleground technique is mixture, producing an enharmonic ♭VI (as E Major) and chromatic neighbor notes to $\hat{3}$ and $\hat{5}$ (♭$\hat{3}$ and ♭$\hat{6}$ as ♮$\hat{2}$ and ♮$\hat{5}$, respectively)—see Ex. 7.5. Register change is the second-middleground device that organizes the swirl of chromatic chords in bars 19-24: the compound tenth great E♮-g#′ in bar 19 moves up an octave by bar 24, beat 1. Chromatic passing tones dominate from that point till the cadence in bars 26-27, followed by neighbor notes in the pedal-point extension of the cadential harmony. (This short passage is used again at the end of the second digression; it also introduces the idea of a minor-subdominant embellishing chord, which is exploited in the final reprise.) The transition is effected mainly with chromatic passing tones, which lead to the db″ neighbor that begins the rondo theme.

Two additional features of detail in the first digression are worth mentioning, if only to show how closely one can interpret motivic features in this Prelude. Both refer to bar 19. First, the chord presented there is a dominant seventh chord on E, which will be the eventual main tonic of the section. This is directly related to bar 4: in both instances, what one might reasonably expect to be the first unequivocal presentation of a root-position tonic of a key region is diverted to secondary or applied dominant status. Second, note that the controlling third-line g#″-f#″-e♮″ (the middleground fundamental line of this section, so to speak) is presaged in the detail of the final three notes of the right hand in bar 19.

EXAMPLE 7.5 The first digression

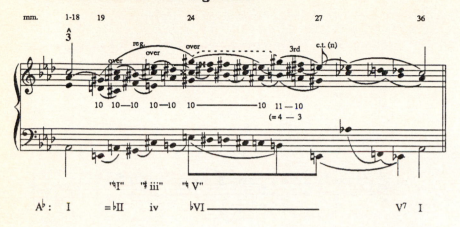

The first reprise of the rondo theme (bars 35-42) gives only the antecedent phrase-pair, so that the second digression may be understood to act within the tonal structure as a prolongation of an interruption (see Ex. 7.6). Except for the pedal-point passage cited above, this digression uses new material, which still bears a close family resemblance to the material of the first digression. The underlying motives are the same. Again a register change organizes

EXAMPLE 7.6 The first reprise and second digression

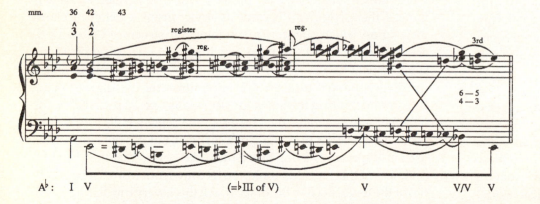

chromatic motions in the first part (b♮'-b♮'' in bars 43-51), chromatic passing tones dominate the approach to the cadence (bars 51-55), the descent to the cadence is a diatonic third-line (bars 55-57), and the pedal-point passage with its iv$^6_4$ follows. (It is by no means impossible, by the way, that the double neighbor notes of bars 43-44 and 47-48 might derive from the pedal-point embellishments of bar 28 or 30.)

The situation at bar 57 (and following) is particularly interesting. Among other things, it shows in a direct way the compositional consequences of the arrangement of the hands in the first bar of the piece. Here, the cadence has led to e♭'', which remains the top voice till it drops out in bar 63. This is of course the cover tone $\hat{5}$. The b♭' below is the $\hat{2}$ of the interruption (from bar 42) and thus represents $\hat{3}$ or c''. It's to this b♭' that the prominent neighbor note c♭'' is applied, the figure being doubled in the lower octave as well. When the e♭'' ceases, the b♭' or $\hat{2}$ is left to itself for three bars, certainly the simplest possible way of prolonging an interruption! Perhaps this lulls the listener into a false sense of security, for what happens next is a surprise: the final reprise is set throughout on a tonic pedal point.[1] The emotional or dramatic curve of the Prelude is thus worked out in a brilliant and satisfying way, one worthy of a much larger composition.

---

[1] This is not precisely what happens in fact: the pedal point contra A♭ is missing in every second bar, but it seems unlikely that any listener would deny that Chopin succeeds in the effect of a continuous pedal-point construction.

Harmonic structure in the reprise is very easy to interpret; melodic structure is not. It might be possible to bring the fundamental line to its close in bar 66, with a♭′. In that case, there would be no interruption, but a long, leisurely descent from 3̂ at the beginning, to 2̂ at bar 42, to 1̂ at bar 66. The remaining bars, then, would serve the normal role of the coda in Schenkerian theory: foreground or later middleground amplification of previous events.

But this explanation seems unsatisfying, since bars 42 and following sound very much like a typical interruption expanding 2̂ over V, and the reprise is clearly more than a coda. A direct descent c″-b♭′-a♭′ in bars 83-84 is much better (see Ex. 7.7, a background/middleground graph of the whole Prelude). Admittedly, this fails to follow the rule that tones of the fundamental line should have harmonic support whenever possible (this is especially true of the tones of the "short" fundamental line from 3̂). It has the further problem that c″ is not literally restated in bar 66 (which is where it should be)—only c′ appears. (The c″ of bar 65 is a passing tone.) In any case, one has to separate the upper octave from the lower: c′ ends the piece as it began it, though now it is free to indulge in reminiscences of the figures it generated (the 2̂ of the interruption appears as a neighbor note b♭ in bars 84-87; a final d♭′ is in bar 89).

(Two harmonic details in the reprise should be mentioned: the harmonies of the rondo theme have been simplified to include nothing but chords on the tonic, dominant, and subdominant: I, V⁷/IV; V and V⁷; IV, iv. The use of the minor subdominant in bars 79-82 strongly suggests what the listener probably already suspects: that the idea for the tonic pedal point of the final reprise came from the pedal-point extensions of the two digressions.)

Felix Salzer has written that "the structural...framework represents the fundamental motion to the goal; it shows the...shortest way to this goal. The whole interest and tension of a piece consists in the expansions, modifications, detours and elaborations of this basic direction...the prolongations.... In the reciprocity between structure and prolongation lies the organic coherence of a musical work" (*Structural Hearing*, p. 14). This "structural framework" is the funda-

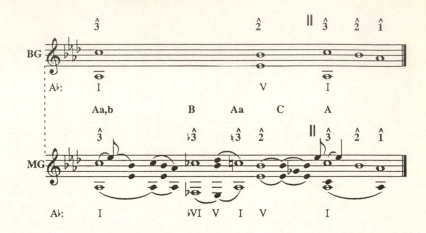

EXAMPLE 7.7 Graph of the entire Prelude

mental structure; the prolongations are all the features of the structural levels resulting from composing-out. These features may be harmonic, melodic, contrapuntal, motivic, registral, formal, rhythmic, or metric, and the ways in which these aspects may be combined or emphasized are myriad.

Chopin's A♭-Major Prelude reveals what we might call a typically nineteenth-century concern for register and motive, where motives which are essentially melodic directly influence harmony, and harmonies themselves can become motivic. From a detail of chord disposition which suggests a fundamental structure (3̂ below 5̂) arises a neighbor note (4̂) from which arise in turn an emphasis on subdominant harmony and the neighbor note (with mixture) as a middleground structural feature that controls the two digressions. A foreground figure in the first digression adds a pedal point below the neighbor and generates the idea of a final reprise built over a tonic pedal. This result is something of a surprise, but it is not hard for the listener (especially having heard the coda) to find that the pulsating calmness of this repeated tonic, too, is drawn out from the possibilities of the tonic chord in the first bar. All this is very much in line with Schenker's views about music's origins and its motivating forces.

Note on motives and your own analyses: Schenker's theory of melody or motive, although in a number of ways quite attractive, is problematic, like his similar theories of form and rhythm or meter (the root cause being that all give an uncritical priority to tonal or tonal/voice-leading structure). Not every composition will reveal tightly interwoven, exhaustive motivic networks. This would be the ideal, but it adds a layer of difficulty to analysis, too. It is by no means demonstrated in the literature that such a perfect correspondence of all elements and their development exists in all of the masterworks from Bach to Brahms. Most writers—Schenker included—have been content to discuss concealed repetition only informally where it can be drawn into the discussion but without making it a requirement.

While working out an analysis, you should be aware of the possibility of recurring motives, but it is important not to make decisions about the bass or the fundamental line based primarily on a search for the right motives—the convincing progression of harmony and voice leading must come first. On the other hand, a study of motivic development, when appropriate, may be integrated into—and greatly enriched by—Schenkerian tonal and voice-leading analysis.

[EXERCISE II.21]

FURTHER READING

In the published literature, consult first of all Charles Burkhart, "Schenker's 'Motivic Parallelisms'," *Journal of Music Theory* 22 (1978): 145-175.

Motivic design in Schenkerian analysis has often been discussed in more recent literature: see the listings under "Two Topics in Tonal Theory," section II, A, in David Beach, "Schenkerian Theory," *Music Theory Spectrum* 11/1 (1989): 12-13. Three articles we would particularly recommend are:

1. David Beach, "Motive and Structure in the Andante Movement of Mozart's Piano Sonata, K. 545," *Music Analysis* 3 (1984): 227-241.

2. Allen Cadwallader, "Schenker's Unpublished Graphic Analysis of Brahms's Intermezzo op. 117 No. 2: Tonal Structure and Concealed Motivic Repetition," *Music Theory Spectrum* 6 (1984): 1-13.

3. Carl Schachter, "The First Movement of Brahms's Second Symphony: The First Theme and its Consequences," *Music Analysis* 2 (1983): 55-68.

Chapter 8: Fundamental Structures and Formal Design

SCHENKER'S THEORY OF FORM

Form, as traditionally conceived, is secondary to tonal structure in Schenker's view. To him, form derives from composing-out and is, in fact, the result of melodic or contrapuntal processes:

> In the music of the early contrapuntal epoch, including even Palestrina, the basic voice-leading events, such as passing tones or neighboring notes, had not yet come to fruition, like flowers in bud. Who would have suspected, at that time, that these phenomena, through the process of diminution, were to become form-generative and would give rise to entire sections and large forms! Although the art of prolongation and diminution ultimately expanded and enriched the form, it was the force of the first passing tone, the first neighboring note, the power of the first structural division which bound form to take on organic unity; and the composer had to make these inner necessities of the background his own.

> *(Free Composition, p. 128)*

Thus, "form [is] the ultimate manifestation of that structural coherence which grows out of background, middleground, and foreground" and "all forms appear in the ultimate foreground; but all of them have their origin in, and derive from, the background" (p. 130). Therefore, we must make a distinction between "inner form" and "outer form," categories we have already referred to in Chapter 3 under the section "Simple Binary Form (Tonic)." This extraordinary reversal of the traditional role of formal design is possible only because Schenker gives priority to composing-out and its attendant tonal structure. He has no interest in motives, themes, or sections as primary form determinants:

> I reject those definitions. . .which take the motive as their starting point and emphasize manipulation of the motive by means of repetition, variation, extension, fragmentation, or dissolution. I also reject those explanations which are based upon phrases, phrase-groups, periods, double periods, themes, antecedents, and consequents. My theory replaces all of these with specific concepts of form which. . .are based upon the content of the whole and of the individual parts; that is, the differences in prolongations lead to differences in form. (p. 131)

We may refer to this as a concept of "generative form"; that is, the interplay of harmony, voice leading, and motive in such a way that a uniquely organic, consequential form results, giving inherent meaning to the usual sectional articulations of familiar formal design stereotypes.

Schenker does not actually discard traditional formal design types. Instead, he radically reinterprets traditional form theory, grouping designs according to the character and disposition of the fundamental line. Thus, he constructs ideal form categories analogous to the ideal tonal structures of the fundamental structure; traditional form design types are simply surface manifestations of these ideal forms. Much of the interpretation of "inner form" is based on the presence or absence of two of the most common features of the first middleground: interruption and mixture. Forms are classified according to the number of divisions generated by these middleground phenomena.

Schenker recognizes designs with one to five parts. Undivided or one-part form has an "undivided progression of the fundamental line." Two pieces we examined in Chapter 5, the chorale "Du Friedensfürst" and the Prelude in C Major from the Well-Tempered Clavier, are one-part forms, even though they are entirely different in terms of their "outer form." It is even possible for a binary-form dance to have an undivided "inner form." For example, in a dance with a fundamental line from $\hat{5}$, the A-section may end on the tonic, and the line may avoid descending to $\hat{2}$ with interruption in B1. Despite the section repetitions (which Schenker says are very important but which, nevertheless, fail to influence the essential tonal structure), the fundamental line in such a piece will be undivided. As Schenker has it, the sensitive or knowledgeable listener will recognize that psychologically the form is one-part, since the binary division arises rather late in the composing-out process.

The two-part and three-part forms are closely related. Two-part form usually arises from interruption—many pieces in the familiar binary forms would conform to this model. Still, a one-to-one correspondence between the two parts of the "inner form" and sections A and B of the "outer form" is very rare. With three-part forms, the "inner" and "outer form" will more often coincide. These designs may arise by various means, including interruption, mixture, or neighbor notes. In the first case, the middle section is built on a prolongation of the $\hat{2}$ over V; in the latter two cases, on mixture or an upper neighbor note to the first tone of the fundamental line. The traditional sonata form, to be discussed later in this chapter, is a special type of three-part form in which interruption is obligatory (the three parts are not exposition, development, and recapitulation, but descent of the fundamental line to the interruption, prolongation of the interruption, and complete and final descent of the fundamental line). Schenker also recognizes a four-part form (A-B-A-B; sometimes erroneously called "sonatina form") and a five-part form which is the basis of the rondo.

FUNDAMENTAL STRUCTURES AND BINARY AND TERNARY FORMS

Schenker's categories of "inner forms" have great conceptual value, but their practical use is limited. Therefore, we will continue to work as we have earlier with models for binary and ternary forms, showing how elements of the fundamental structure may be distributed within them. In general, be aware of the "inner form" of a composition you analyze, but focus on it only for comparison purposes; that is, to relate it to other pieces which may have the same "inner form" but different "outer forms."[1]

An important difference obtains between the models in Chapter 3 and those presented below. The latter cannot be relied on to account directly or precisely, down to the placement of individual tones, for the majority of pieces with these designs. Events of the middleground can be quite varied and will often displace tones of the fundamental line, sometimes even the bass arpeggiation, so that the models below should be regarded only as the simplest possibilities, not necessary solutions into which every composition must be forced to fit.

The models given here are those proper to eighteenth-century binary and ternary forms; many others can easily be referred to these. The sonata, for example, depends on the patterns of the binary form. The rondo, dance pairs, da capo aria, and many nineteenth-century character pieces depend on the ternary form. And so on.

The simplest binary forms, tonic and dominant types, with or without reprise, and with a fundamental line from $\hat{3}$, appear in Ex. 8.1. The corresponding minor-key models are shown in Ex. 8.2. For those relatively few pieces in the major key in which section A closes on iii (or III), the notation may be borrowed from the minor key models, as in Ex. 8.3. Note that all the models in Exs. 8.1-8.3 are two-part "inner forms" because of the interruption, but remember that the disposition of the two parts depends not on the standard binary-design sections but on the placement of the interruption. For instance, in the first model in Ex. 8.1, the first part of the "inner form" encompasses sections A1, A2, and B1; the second part is B2.

---

[1] Even making this allowance, there are some forms or genres which remain difficult to assess, either because they have not been adequately treated in the literature yet (such as many eighteenth-century vocal forms or the Baroque and Classical concerto) or because of inherent difficulties (such as the polyphonic genres, in particular fugue). On the latter, see Susan Tepping, "Fugue Process and Tonal Structure in the String Quartets of Haydn, Mozart, and Beethoven," Ph.D. dissertation, Indiana University, 1987.

EXAMPLE 8.1 Binary forms, tonic and
dominant, with or without reprise; major
key; fundamental line from 3̂

EXAMPLE 8.2 Binary forms, tonic and
dominant, with or without reprise; minor
key; fundamental line from 3̂

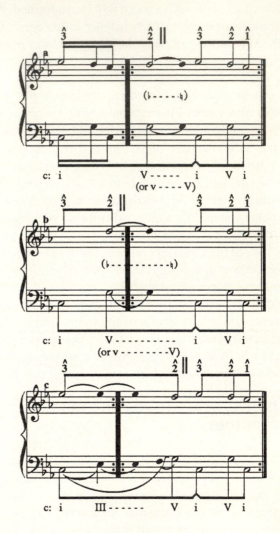

Examples in the literature: In *Free Composition* : Figs. 35,1 (Mozart); 35,2 Mozart); 40,1 (Chopin); 82,2 (Beethoven). In *Structural Hearing*: Figs. 494-495 (two unusual examples of undivided "inner form" in the binary frame, from Bach and Brahms—could either of these have been read with interruption?). In *The Book of the Musical Artwork*: Bach, Violin Partita in E, Menuet; Haydn, Sonata in C minor, II.

Some typical models for binary forms, tonic and dominant types, with the fundamental line from 5̂ are illustrated in Exs. 8.4 (major key) and 8.5 (minor key). The first model includes two features found again and again, not only in this type of composition but also in many others where the interruption occurs: 1) a second-order fifth line descending from 2̂ and creating a degree of closure for the first section; 2) a cover-tone-like anticipation of the 5̂ before the latter's return over I.

EXAMPLE 8.3 Binary forms, mediant, with or without reprise; major key; fundamental line from 3̂

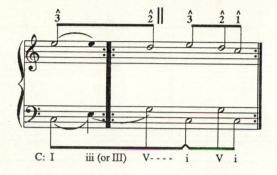

C: I   iii (or III)   V - - - - i   V   i

The third model is a variant of the second; it shows two upper parts—a "structural soprano" on 5̂ and a "structural alto" on 3̂. The latter is actually a part of the middleground (that is, not a part of the essential two-part counterpoint of the fundamental structure) but its inclusion is often useful in pieces where there is clear emphasis on 2̂ but no descent from 5̂.

Examples in the literature: In *Free Composition*: Figs. 40,9 (Paganini); 103,6 (Handel); 152,4 (J.S. Bach). In Forte and Gilbert: Exs. 143 and 179 (Handel; undivided form; follows the third model in Ex. 8.4); 155 (Mozart); 180 (Bach). In *Structural Hearing*: Fig. 475 (Mozart; rounded binary design; minor key). In *The Book of the Musical Artwork*: Mozart, Menuet in F; Sonata in A, K. 331, I, theme.

The fundamental line from 8̂ is much less common than the others, and it is easy to see why: when set into a formal design, it is rather cumbersome (see Ex. 8.6). Still, some pieces must be referred to this model, as we have seen in Chapter 5 with Bach's Invention in G Major. The models show the division of the line at 5̂—this is the octave-line's substitute for interruption. In the division, 5̂ is first reached over V and is prolonged as the bass moves to I, after which the line continues its descent. We might add that compositions with a fundamental line from 8̂ are found mostly in the Baroque repertoire.

EXAMPLE 8.4 Binary forms, tonic and dominant, with or without reprise; major key; fundamental line from 5̂

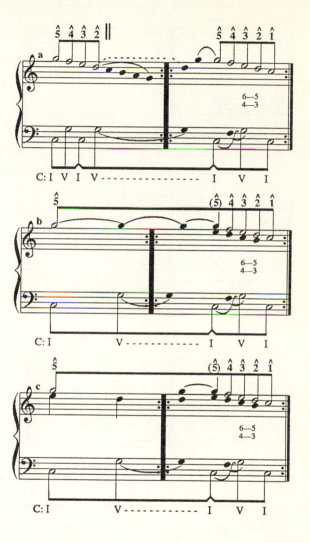

Examples in the literature: In *Free Composition*: Figs. 20,4 (Mozart); 47,3 (J.S. Bach); 76,4 (J.S. Bach). In Forte and Gilbert, see pp.180-184.

EXAMPLE 8.5 Binary forms, tonic and dominant, with or without reprise; minor key; fundamental line from $\hat{5}$

EXAMPLE 8.6 Binary forms, tonic and dominant, with or without reprise; major key; fundamental line from $\hat{8}$

If we take the simplest possibility for the ternary designs—a fundamental line from 3̂ with an A B A design where A is tonally closed and B is on the dominant—, the result would be something like Ex. 8.7. (Ex. 8.7a is the preferred reading; Ex. 8.7b provides an alternate.) Here, the descent to the tonic at the end of the first A section is relegated to the middleground and section B is assigned the 2̂, and interruption. Common models for the ternary design in the minor key (fundamental line from 3̂) and the major key (fundamental line from 5̂) are shown in Ex. 8.8. Interruption is the most common feature, but a first-middleground neighbor note or mixture can be the primary generator of the B-section.

EXAMPLE 8.7 Ternary forms; major key; fundamental line from 3̂

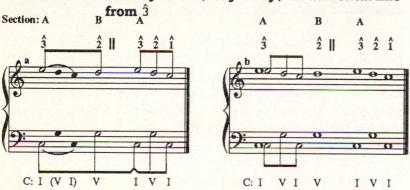

EXAMPLE 8.8 Ternary forms; major key (5̂); minor key (3̂)

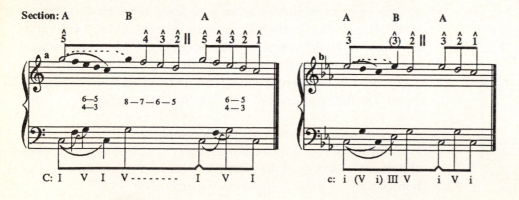

In general, the procedures applied to the binary/ternary form also apply to the simple ternary design, and the models shown here apply, by extension, to compound ternary forms (such as the menuet and trio) or rondos. A first middleground graph for a rondeau by Bach appears in Ex. 8.9. Note that the first digression includes III and motion toward an interruption (rather than being formed by prolongation of an interruption occurring at the beginning) and that the second digression is created by a neighbor-note motion (3̂-4̂-3̂).

EXAMPLE 8.9 J. S. Bach, English Suite no. 6, Passepied. Background/first middleground graph

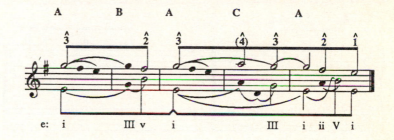

Examples in the literature: In *Free Composition*, see pp. 132-133 (§310) and the figures mentioned there, especially Figs. 22,b (Schumann); 30,a (Chopin); 30,b (Schubert); 46,1 (Brahms); 76,3 (Chopin); 153,1 (Chopin); 153,2 (Chopin); 153,3 (Chopin). In Forte and Gilbert: Exs. 183 (Brahms); 184 (Schumann); and Chapter 23. In *Structural Hearing*: Figs. 499 (Chopin; interruption at the end of B); 500 (Chopin; B as prolongation of an interruption); 502 (Schubert; unusual treatment of neighbor-note to generate B). In *The Book of the Musical Artwork*: Mendelssohn, "Spinning Song"; Schumann, Romance in F♯, op. 28, no. 2.

SONATA FORM

To Schenker, as to many others in his generation and before, Vienna was the center of all music, Beethoven its king, and the sonata its queen. Not surprisingly, then, the discussion of sonata form takes up a major portion of the otherwise brief and rather elliptical form chapter in *Free Composition*. Exs. 8.10 and 8.11 below illustrate the basic components of the tonal/voice-leading structure of typical sonata movements in the major key, with fundamental lines from $\hat{3}$ or $\hat{5}$.

EXAMPLE 8.10 Model for a sonata movement, major key, line from $\hat{3}$

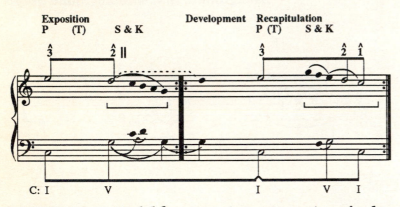

EXAMPLE 8.11 Model for a sonata movement, major key, line from $\hat{5}$

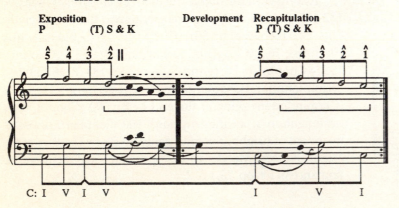

Schenker accepts the three main divisions, exposition, development, and recapitulation, but he labels them the main section, the middle section, and the repetition, and he has his own view of their proper contents. The exposition or main section has two essential prolongations—in Ex. 8.10, these are $\hat{3}$ over I and $\hat{2}$ over V. The entire range of possibilities exists to prolong the former, but the prolongation of $\hat{2}$ over V is a middleground fifth-line in the key region of V (shown with a bracket in the example). Schenker says of this that "it is designated by conventional theory as the second theme. . .or the like . . .Once more I must emphasize that these are in every respect inadequate terms and concepts which afford no insight into sonata form." He insists that "a fifth-progression in itself suffices for the prolongation of [$\hat{2}$ over V] without necessarily involving a 'lyrical' or 'contrasting' theme" (*Free Composition*, p. 135).

Of course, none of this applies to second-theme areas in the mediant or other non-dominant key region. In such cases, the prolonged first tone of the fundamental line or a middleground neighbor note is the controlling structural feature, though a descending line will typically also lead from it. Last-moment moves to the dominant in a first ending are usually ignored.

Schenker also rejects the sense of "working out" for the development or middle section; instead, its "only obligation, according to the structural division, is to complete the motion to [$\hat{2}$ over V][or in some way to expand that point]" (p. 136). Thus, in the models, the development is shown simply as a later middleground extension of $\hat{2}$ over V. One feature which does occur with some regularity is a "late" middleground line starting from some dominant chord tone and moving to the $\hat{2}$ (or sometimes $\hat{4}$, as the seventh of V^7). In sonatas where the exposition ends in the mediant, the development either reaches $\hat{2}$ over V quickly and then prolongs it or, more commonly, reaches the $\hat{2}$ over V in the "retransition" near the end of the section.

The recapitulation or repetition accomplishes "the closure of the fundamental line and the bass arpeggiation" (p. 137). The distribution of elements is shown in the example, with the bracket showing the transposition of the fifth-line from the exposition.

This concept of the sonata form has a number of points to recommend it. First, it is sufficiently broad to account for almost any sonata movement written in the eighteenth or nineteenth centuries, including those without clearly defined second themes, those without "proper" developments or recapitulations, and even those with unusual tonal schemes. Second, it is consistent with many twentieth-century views of the sonata as an organic and dramatic form; in fact, a "drama of tonalities." Finally, it is consistent with later eighteenth-century and some nineteenth-century descriptions, which emphasize main divisions and tonal structure but not themes or theme areas.

For our purposes, then, the sonata form poses few special problems other than the luxuriance of detail which one will find in any composition of substantial length. The models of the binary designs apply directly to the sonata, only in expanded form, and the variants are not so many as one might think from the size of the repertoire.

The traditional main-theme area contains any initial-ascent pattern and at least the first tone of the fundamental line, which may be from $\hat{3}$ or $\hat{5}$ (but not $\hat{8}$ because of the problem of fitting the $\hat{8}$-line's division into the formal design). The main-theme area or subsequent transition will contain a descent to $\hat{2}$ over V. The distribution of elements can vary considerably, but those things listed above will occur. Rarely, the descent to $\hat{2}$ occurs in the second-theme area, and it is, of course, lacking when the second theme is in the mediant, as in many sonatas in the minor key, for example.

The first movement of Beethoven, Piano Sonata, op. 14, no. 2, shows a characteristic treatment of the opening (see Ex. 8.12). An initial ascent leads from g' to b' (the $\hat{3}$), and the interruption occurs relatively early in the transition. (Our reading of this movement is based on Schenker's analysis in *Free Composition*, Figs. 47,2 and 154,6.)

The second theme and closing theme prolong the $\hat{2}$ over V with the middleground fifth-line from $\hat{2}$: $\hat{2}$-$\hat{1}$-$\hat{7}$-$\hat{6}$-$\hat{5}$. The second part of the exposition of op. 14, no. 2, in Ex. 8.13, in fact, shows two of these lines, the first from a'' in bars 26-44, the second from a' in bar 48, which arises from coupling of the earlier a''.

EXAMPLE 8.12 Beethoven, Piano Sonata, op. 14, no. 2, I, opening

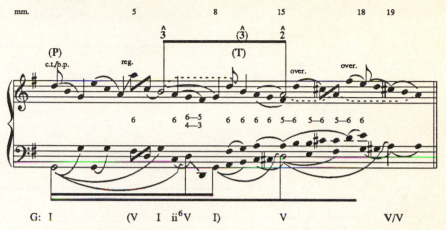

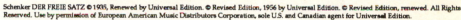

The development section continues the prolongation of $\hat{2}$ over V and is usually interpreted as consisting almost entirely of foreground elaboration in the form of lines, mixture, register changes, and so on, in unpredictable arrangements. It is almost always best to begin analysis of a development section with a detailed bass-line sketch. This will establish the harmonic progressions and functional hierarchies involved and make interpretation of the upper parts much easier.

Three examples of sonata developments are given in *Free Composition*, Figs. 154, 5-7, including the development of op. 14, no. 2, I (Fig. 154,6). About this, Schenker writes: "As in the previous example [Beethoven, Symphony no. 6, I], a seventh is transferred upward (V8-7—here, however, in a different way" (p. 137). A reading of this development is given in Ex. 8.14. This reading differs from Schenker's in a number of details, but also in including another feature (in addition to the transferred seventh) at the same level; that is, a fourth-line from the cover tone d'' downward to a recurrence of the $\hat{2}$ of the interruption (as d''-c''-b♭'-a'—note that this motion produces parallel fifths with the bass). (Note: Salzer devotes an entire section of a chapter to the sonata development (*Structural Hearing*, pp. 210-216).)

EXAMPLE 8.13 op. 14, no. 2, I, second part of the exposition

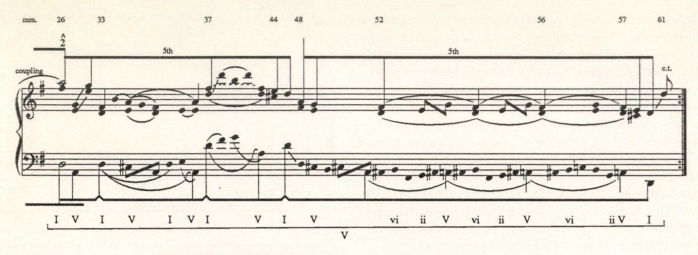

The reprise re-establishes the fundamental line after the interruption. The descent of the fundamental line will normally occur at the end of the second-theme area, sometimes in the closing theme, rarely in a coda. Codas are in most cases to be regarded as foreground or late middleground extensions of the final tone of the fundamental line. In minor-key sonatas where the second and closing themes are recapitulated in the parallel major key, mixture is applied.

A middleground reading of the entire first movement of op. 14, no. 2, appears in Ex. 8.15, showing, among other things, how the second theme's fifth-line (shown in brackets) is treated in the exposition and recapitulation. When the fundamental line is from $\hat{3}$, the fifth-line in the recapitulation must be split into two thirds—in bars 152 ff., d''-c''-b' and b'-a'-g'. With the line from $\hat{5}$, this problem does not arise.

Readings: Schenker's discussion of sonata form begins on p. 133 of *Free Composition*. The translator, Ernst Oster, has added an extended, very useful footnote on anomalous sonata designs, pp. 139-141. An earlier essay from *Meisterwerk*, vol. 2, "Organic Structure in Sonata Form," appears translated in Maury Yeston, ed., *Readings in Schenker Analysis...*, p. 38.

Other examples: In *Five Graphic Music Analyses*: Haydn (development section only). In Forte and Gilbert: Chapter 21 (three extended examples, two from Haydn, one from Beethoven). In *Structural Hearing*: Fig. 497 (Schubert; extended minor-key example); also, 475 (Mozart; rounded binary design indistinguishable from a compact sonata movement; the same piece is discussed as "sonatina form" in Forte and Gilbert, pp. 213 ff.). In *The Book of the Musical Artwork*: Mozart, Sonata in C, K. 545, I; Beethoven, Sonata in G minor, op. 49, no. 1, I.
[EXERCISES II.18; II.19; II.20; Essays in II.22-25]

EXAMPLE 8.14 op. 14, no. 2, I, development section

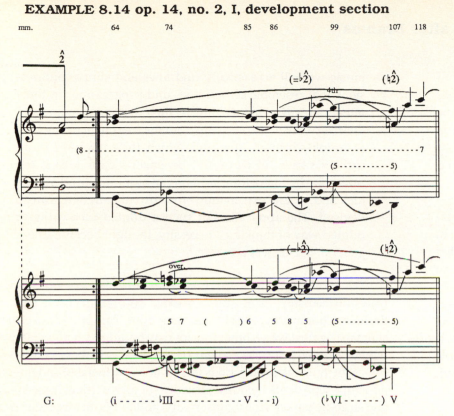

EXAMPLE 8.15 op. 14, no. 2, I, entire movement

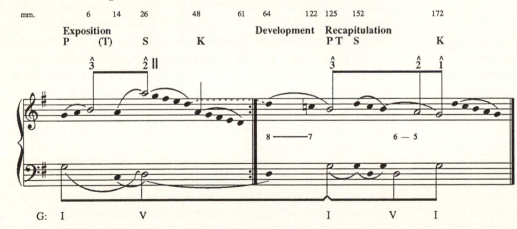

111

Chapter 9: Analysis of Music before Bach and after Brahms

In this chapter we explore subjects which are at the periphery of Schenkerian theory and analytic practice: the highly chromatic music of the later nineteenth century and the specialized repertoires of the seventeenth century (or earlier) and of the twentieth century. Even though these musics were not within Schenker's immediate range of interests, he did write about them and some of his own students and followers have explored them using extensions of his methods.

Schenker was by no means reticent about expressing a patronizing pity for the still unperfected music of composers before Bach. In Chapter 8, for example, we cited a passage from *Free Composition* that refers to Palestrina and his contemporaries as composers who were not yet able to take the elements of detail in their music and create "long lines" of prolongations through composing-out. On the other hand, Schenker harbored anger and disdain at the decadence of twentieth-century music. He analyzed a fragment from Stravinsky's Piano Concerto, apparently in order to show how incomprehensible he found it—the verdict: "Stravinsky's writing is...thoroughly bad, unartistic, and unmusical" (*Meisterwerk,* vol. 2, p. 39).

As we have seen, Schenker believed his method did, in fact, show how the great masters composed, what was the essence of their music and their method. And he obviously assumed that this analytic system was as "organic" as the processes he saw in the music he analyzed. Any change in the balance of the process of composing-out of the tonic triad and the prolongation of strict counterpoint would mean the unacceptable distortion of those principles and the consequent debasement of music. Ernst Oster expresses this point of view succinctly:

Any musical composition. . .would reveal certain connections, even though it had been pieced together in the most dilettantish way. Somewhere some tone is certain to continue to some other tone, and it is therefore easy to discover horizontal lines well-nigh everywhere. Thus, in non-triadic music we will occasionally find lines and simple progressions that resemble certain lines and progressions in tonal music. However, in tonal music, their deepest meaning and their very existence originate from the triad which they help to unfold through time and which they interpret in an endless variety of ways. . . . Schenker's basic idea is the projection in time of the triad as given by nature. Mutilate this idea and. . . .an "explanation" for virtually anything can be devised. The application of such a diluted idea makes a diluted way of thinking a necessity; thought becomes more general, hazier, less accurate.[1]

Schenker held to a view of European music history which limits true musicianship to mostly Germanic composers from Bach to Brahms (Chopin is the one notable exception). This provides a critical standard against which other musics may be judged, a universal and natural standard for assessment of quality (as if these composers represent the ideal for all periods in the same way that the fundamental structure represents the ideal structure of any particular piece). By and large, Schenker's most conservative followers maintain this view even today. Any work you may do with "atypical" repertoires, then, obliges you to react to this notion of history and its derivative critical standard. The basic problem is, Do you simply accept Schenker's concepts and try to "stretch" their application a bit to account for such things as modality or complex chords? Or, do you rethink the concepts of the theory to be appropriate to the style and techniques of the music at hand? In the first case, results are pre-interpreted in terms of Schenker's ideology, no matter how subtle or interesting you find the composition at hand—early music is still imperfect and twentieth-century music is still decadent. The second approach,

---

[1]Ernst Oster, "Re: A New Concept of Tonality (?)," *Journal of Music Theory* 4 (1960): 96-97. Oster's article is a critique of Roy Travis, "Toward a New Concept of Tonality," *Journal of Music Theory* 3 (1959): 257-284.

overall, is more satisfying and likely to lead to better results, but it is also more difficult and is likely to draw the reproach that the analysis is no longer "Schenkerian" (as in the passage from Oster cited above).

In general, we offer two bits of advice for your own work: 1) Carefully justify your methods, either by identifying and following an established model (such as Salzer) or by defining your procedures, especially for such things as background or first middleground structures, linear connections, and prolongation; 2) Make sure that you are stylistically sensitive to the music you are working on and, as much as possible, adjust the analytic tools accordingly.

MUSIC BEFORE BACH

A surprisingly large Schenker-oriented literature exists on music before Bach, much of it written by Felix Salzer or students and associates of his. The central technical question involved in most cases is the treatment of modality. Compositions securely based in the major/minor tonal system, such as the dances in Lully operas and ballets or most Italian instrumental works after about 1680, pose few unusual problems. But modal compositions force the analyst to make a decision: Should one follow the characteristics of the modes, even if that means reading the most basic events of the background and first middleground differently, or should one apply Schenker's method more or less as is? One may encounter plagal structural cadences, modal rather than diatonic lines (even a fundamental line $\hat{4}$-$\hat{3}$-($\flat$)$\hat{2}$-$\hat{1}$ in the Phrygian mode!), increased significance for cadences in the middleground, increased significance for the "species" of octaves, fifths, and fourths appropriate to a mode (more on this below), and the possibility that the fundamental line may not lie in the uppermost voice or the bass arpeggiation in the bass.[2]

---

[2]A tenor-cantus Ursatz was proposed by Frederick Bashour in"A Model for the Analysis of Structural Levels and Tonal Movement in Compositions of the Fifteenth Century," 2 vols, Ph.D. dissertation, Yale University. 1975.

A device proposed by Salzer, the "contrapuntal structure" (abbreviated CS), solves some, but not all, of these problems (it's also useful for non-traditional twentieth-century music). "Chords whose status is clearly contrapuntal [such as a neighbor chord] may assume structural significance. If a contrapuntal chord is used to support a structural tone in the melody, it has the significance of a structural chord"(*Structural Hearing*, pp. 160-161). Later, Salzer says that "even a complete piece may be based on a contrapuntal progression. . . Tonal coherence. . .can thus be expressed in three ways, either through a contrapuntal structure or a harmonic structure or a combination of both" (p. 222).

Bach's setting of the chorale "Christus, der uns selig macht," no. 81 from the "371" will serve to illustrate the contrapuntal structure in a modal composition (see Ex. 9.1). The chorale melody is written in the Phrygian mode (final or "tonic" E); this setting is used to open Part II of the *St. John Passion*. The melody has eight phrases, divided by the rhyme scheme and grammatical structure of the text into two units of four phrases each.

The fundamental line is an octave, e''-e', with the Phrygian $\hat{2}$ (f$\natural$'). The harmonization produces a completely contrapuntal structure (see the middleground graph in Ex. 9.2). A "harmonic structure" would be based on functional patterns, I-V-I or I-ii-V-I; these are entirely absent here, and we have instead a harmonic pattern which emphasizes iv and which, overall, is based on the progression, Phrygian: I-iv-VI-vii-I. Functional harmonic progressions only begin to appear in the later middleground.

To judge from Salzer's own examples, the contrapuntal support of an extended line such as this is rare. Neighboring or brief linear progressions would be more likely, such as third-lines, or contrapuntal chords within a more extended harmonic structure (see *Structural Hearing*, Figs. 318-323, 478-480). On the other hand, compositions in the Phrygian mode typically give strong emphasis to degrees $\hat{4}$ and $\hat{6}$, in both melody and harmony; these act as "substitutes" for the $\hat{5}$, which may be important in melody but never in harmony.

EXAMPLE 9.1 Chorale, "Christus, der uns selig macht" in J. S. Bach's setting

EXAMPLE 9.2 "Christus, der uns selig macht," Analysis using Salzer's contrapuntal structure (CS)

Our second example is another chorale in Bach's setting, "Mach's mit mir, Gott, nach deiner Güt'." In this case we will concentrate on the species of octaves and their subdivisions into species of fifths and fourths. Most scholars agree that these constitute the essential starting point for an effective analysis of modal music. Thus, we assert that the natural tonal space for the sixteenth and seventeenth-century chorale repertoire is the octave, subdivided into fifth and fourth (1̂-5̂, 5̂-8̂ or 5̂-8̂, 1̂-5̂; but in some circumstances also 1̂-4̂, 4̂-8̂ or 4̂-8̂, 1̂-4̂). Chorale melodies present a wide range of patterns possible within these distinct tonal "subspaces," including lines, neighbor-note patterns, and so on.

A reading of "Mach's mit mir. . ." and its setting is given in Ex. 9.3. The first level (at the top) is a tonal/spatial ("TS") background/

middleground. At the far left is a composite view of the tonal space of the melody (treble clef) and of the harmony in Bach's setting (bass). This tonal space functions as the equivalent of fundamental structure for the chorale (treble alone) or the setting (treble and bass). The remainder of the treble clef is a middleground-level view of the essential presentations of the species within the tonal space of the octave. The melody is in mode 11 (or Ionian), but the transposition level of Bach's setting has been used here to make comparison easier; the octave is, thus, divided into the fifth d'-a' and the fourth a'-d".

The second level of Ex. 9.3 is a spatial/linear middleground ("SL 1"), which shows a large-scale linear motion, rising and falling through the octave d'-d" and weaving its way through the middleground fifth/fourth species. (The "tremolo" marking on e' in

115

EXAMPLE 9.3 Chorale, "Mach's mit mir, Gott, nach deiner Güt' " and J. S. Bach's setting: Analysis using the modal species of octaves, fifths, and fourths

phrase 3 indicates that the fifth species is incomplete—the e' substitutes for d'.) The symmetry of rising and falling lines and their steady progress through the fifth/fourth species in both first and second phrases is also evident on the larger scale of the entire chorale. A striking and somewhat unusual feature revealed by this level is the greater relative stability of the fourth, a'-d''. The fifth, d'-a', is unsettled by the repeated commixture of the fourth e'-a'. ("Commixture" refers to the introduction of species from a different mode; here, the fourth e'-a' properly belongs to a (transposed) mode whose final is A.) The symmetrical design of the melody is enhanced even further by the fact that the pitch which completes the fifth, d', appears only twice—as the first and last notes.

The third level, "SL 2," is a foreground which has the content of the previous levels plus some additional information. Note in particular the confusion in the final phrase, which necessitates two readings of the fifth/fourth species and allows two readings of the linear design as well.

The fourth and final level is a tonal/spatial/linear ("TSL") reading which includes SL 2 as interpreted by Bach's setting and a bass-line sketch showing major/minor harmonic functions. Tonic harmony strongly supports the first fifth species, d'-a', but the fourth, a'-d'', is effectively reduced to a third with neighbor note (see the inset above the graph) because of dominant support. This is not what we might have expected from the structure of the melody and is clearly forceful interpretation on Bach's part. In the second section, the commixture is reduced to an inner-voice diminution by the subdominant-

116

dominant functional sequence (again, see the inset), and the ambivalence of the final phrase is removed by a decision which clearly marks the first pair, g′-f♯′, as the descent, $\hat{4}$-$\hat{3}$.[3]

We recommend the following from the literature on music before Bach as starting points for your own investigations:

1. Saul Novack, "The Analysis of Pre-Baroque Music," in *Aspects of Schenkerian Theory*, pp. 113-133.

2. Felix Salzer, "Heinrich Schenker and Historical Research: Monteverdi's Madrigal Oimè, se tanto amate," in *Aspects of Schenkerian Theory*, pp. 135-152.

3. Adele Katz, *Challenge to Musical Tradition* (New York 1945).

4. Peter Bergquist, "Mode and Polyphony around 1500," *Music Forum* 1 (1967): 99-161.

5. William J. Mitchell, "The Prologue to Orlando di Lasso's *Prophetiae Sibyllarum*," *Music Forum* 2 (1970): 264-273.

6. Miguel Roig-Francoli, "Compositional Theory and Practice in Mid-sixteenth Century Castilian Instrumental Music: The *Arte de tañer fantasia* by Tomás de Santa María and the Music of Antonio de Cabezón," Ph.D. dissertation, Indiana University, 1990.

---

[3]Compare the analysis given here with those in Neumeyer, "The Urlinie from $\hat{8}$ as a Middleground Phenomenon," *In Theory Only* 9/5-6 (1987): 3-25; David Beach, "The Fundamental Line from Scale Degree 8: Criteria for Evaluation," *Journal of Music Theory* 32/2 (1988): 271-294; and Neumeyer, "Fragile Octaves, Broken Lines: On Some Limitations in Schenkerian Theory and Practice," *In Theory Only* 11/3 (1989): 11-30.

MUSIC AFTER BRAHMS

Three major issues are involved for Schenkerian analysis of late-nineteenth and twentieth-century music: 1) expanded chord vocabulary; 2) extended functional usage; and 3) prolongational procedures in non-traditional tonal (and "atonal") music.

Of these, the expansion of chord vocabulary is the easiest to deal with. Increasing attention to chromatic key regions, beginning with the chromatic mediants in the early nineteenth century, was followed mainly in the second half of the century by a gradual increase in the acceptable dissonant sonorities. The dominant ninth chord (whose existence Schenker rejected, by the way) was firmly established as an independent sonority by about 1860. With a few exceptions (mainly for dances such as the waltz), it is not appropriate to describe apparent dominant-ninth constructions as harmonic in music before this time—they are melodic phenomena still based on the 9-8 suspension figure. More complex chords (elevenths and thirteenths) did not become true harmonies until about 1890. Not long before, roughly 1860-1870, major triads with added sixths also became legitimate sonorities. The triads to which sixths were added are I, IV, V, and iv in the main key or secondary key regions. These chords appear only with the root in the bass; the sixth makes a major (not minor) second with the fifth of the triad and, if possible, should appear in the highest voice.

Our example is by Alexander Scriabin: Prelude, op. 15, no. 4 (see the score in Ex. 9.4; graphs in Ex. 9.5). A chordal reduction is included—we strongly recommend this as a basic tool for the analysis of later nineteenth-century music, particularly works like this one, strongly harmonic but often heavily embellished with diminutions. Harmonic rhythm in this Prelude is relatively slow, normally one harmony per bar after the opening pedal-point tonic. In the detailed figuration hide several complex sonorities (extended tertian chords), presented in arpeggiated forms with considerable doubling; few of these survive as actual harmonies in the chordal reduction. The bass, as usual in such cases, provides the best clues to harmonic and tonal motion, and the apparent complexity resolves itself into quite a

EXAMPLE 9.4 Alexander Scriabin: Prelude, op. 15, no. 4

straightforward (and traditionally triadic) foreground and middleground with a first-order interruption and chromatic motion in the prolongation of the $\hat{2}$ over V (bars 8 ff.).

Harmony was a musical element that particularly fascinated nineteenth-century composers, and the interplay between powerful harmonic patterning and voice leading, on both local and larger levels, is one of the constants for that repertory. In Scriabin's Prelude, op. 39, no. 2 (Ex. 9.6), we find the more intense chromaticism—though still with a discernible diatonic-functional basis—that was typical of the sometimes dense but free-floating harmonic patterning in music after Wagner.

EXAMPLE 9.5 Alexander Scriabin: Prelude, op. 15, no. 4, analysis graphs

EXAMPLE 9.6 Alexander Scriabin: Prelude, op. 39, no. 2

EXAMPLE 9.7 Alexander Scriabin: Prelude, op. 39, no. 2, analysis graphs

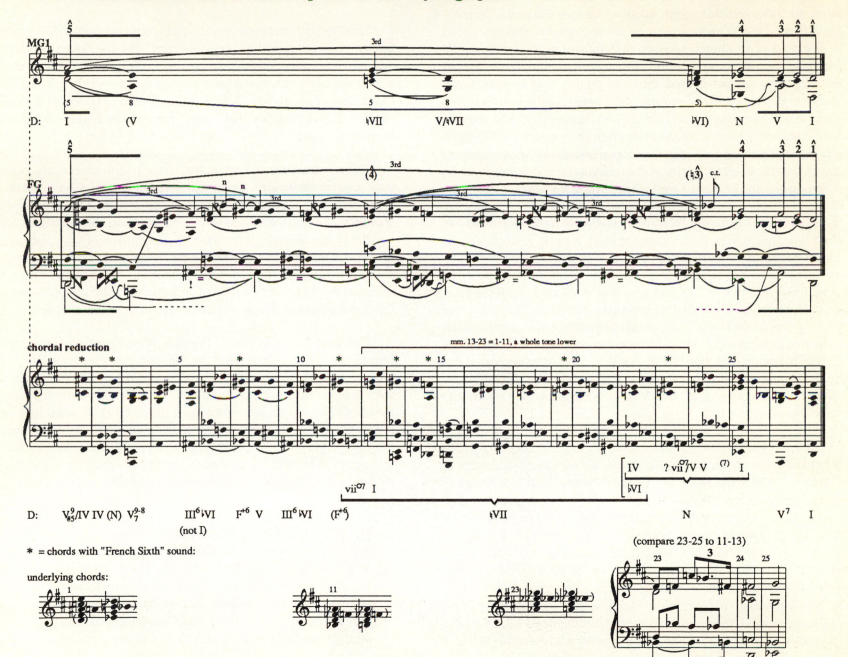

Scriabin derives several of his harmonies from chromatic alteration, such as the striking first chord, which introduces the "French-Sixth" sound that is a special feature of this Prelude—this first chord is best read as an altered secondary dominant of the following IV harmony. We can thus postulate a D-major triad voiced so as to lead correctly through the altered chord to the IV. This implied tonic, shown in brackets at the beginning of the foreground graph, becomes the opening harmony of the background, supporting the $\hat{5}$ that we would plausibly hear as voice-led through a♯' to b' (see Ex. 9.7). Such a procedure is by no means unusual; many later-nineteenth century compositions seem to begin in the middle of things, as it were, continuing logically from a tonic chord we never hear.

This rather unusually "abstract" reading of the background has the advantage that, in this instance at least, it greatly simplifies our understanding of the composition's essential features. The middleground 1 graph shows an unproblematic fundamental structure with a line from $\hat{5}$ and a full harmonic cycle with the Neapolitan (or Phrygian $\hat{2}$) chord replacing the diatonic ii. The first-order prolongation of the D-major triad is accomplished with a contrapuntal structure (5-8 sequence) supporting a non-diatonic third-line (a'-g'-f'). The harmonic-functional complexities of the score are sorted out by the bass in the foreground graph, which shows somewhat unexpected prolongations of the V and V/VII harmonies in the middleground graph.

Our manner of reading this Prelude is entirely consistent with Schenker's treatment of chromaticism, as we discussed them in Chapter 1, under the heading "Implied Notes," and in Chapter 6, under the headings "Mixture" and "Chromaticism at Later Levels." That is to say, most often, chromatic progressions serve to prolong underlying diatonic chords or tones. In some instances, chromatic chords can be understood to replace a diatonic chord at a later level, and the latter must then be inferred from the harmonic-functional and voice-leading context. We might in fact have chosen this option for the beginning, by placing the D-major triad in background and middleground(s), then substituting for it the altered V^7/IV in the foreground. For situations like this, our usual advice applies: Make a choice based on what seems most appropriate to the context.

This Prelude receives a very different interpretation in Salzer and Schachter, *Counterpoint in Composition*, pp. 464-467. They base their analysis on an extended IV-V-I progression (IV in bar 2; V-I at the end) with a series of chromatic parallel tenths between bar 2 and the Neapolitan chord in bar 25. Our disagreement only serves to demonstrate the difficulties that attend analysis of highly chromatic functional music.

The non-traditional tonal music of the twentieth century poses even greater challenges. Once again we suggest that, as a starting point, you rely on Salzer's "contrapuntal structure," though you should be aware that there is a long-standing debate about the validity of this concept for most twentieth-century music, at the heart of which is the problem of whether prolongation is possible—and if so how it works—in music where the contrapuntal structural chords are often dissonant (this notion of "dissonant prolongation" is what Oster challenges in the quote at the beginning of this chapter).

Our example is Debussy, Prelude "The Engulfed Cathedral" (Book I, no. 10). We discussed the overall design of the bass in Chapter 2. Here, instead of presenting an analysis of the entire composition, we will look only at one passage containing details characteristic of twentieth-century music which uses procedures or sonorities no longer typical of major/minor functional harmony. The score and a foreground graph of bars 40-49 appear in Ex. 9.8. These bars include the transition from the main theme, which ends grandly with the C-major chord in bar 40, to the second theme (bar 47). Note the following features:

1. Blocks of notes have a single, unified function, as if they formed one "note-out-of-several-notes." We have used a long vertical bracket in bars 40 and 42 to show this. The need for the bracket in bar 40 is not immediately obvious—one has to know that the entire main theme has been presented with these massive triads moving in parallel motion; this C-major chord is, thus, a rich doubling of the melody note (c''), not an array of eight separate

EXAMPLE 9.8 Debussy, Prelude "The Engulfed Cathedral" (Book I, no. 10), bars 40-49

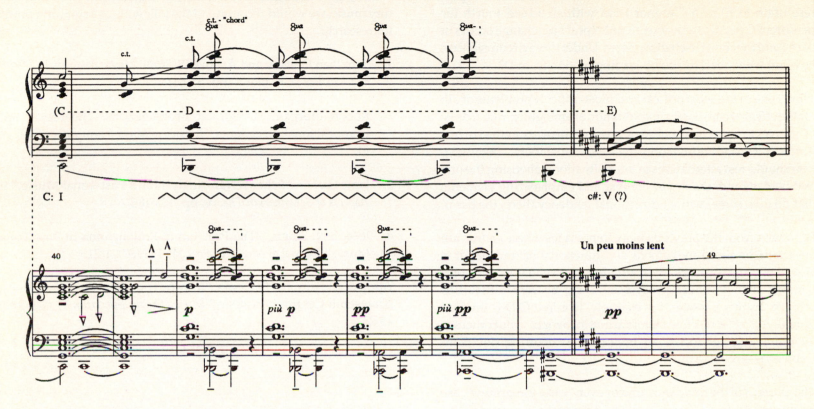

voices in the voice-leading fabric. Similarly, the chord in bar 42 is treated as a (stationary) block of sound, as is the "cover-tone-'chord' " in the highest register.

This device is linked to the increased importance of timbre as a structuring agent in music, and it obliges you to keep in mind that not all notes will necessarily be part of voice-leading progressions.

2. Harmonic function can be attentuated, creating a kind of harmonic patterning in which functionality comes in and out of focus, as it were. Here, the bass moves from the stable and long-held pedal point C toward a similar pedal-point on G♯. There is no doubt that C is the tonic of C major (though one has to account for a few

"modal" inflections); the G♯ is not quite so clear, but from context we can be satisfied that it serves as the V of a C♯ minor whose tonic is never sounded. The path from C to G♯ is not a functional modulation, but purely bass-movement by whole-step; the chord above B♭ simply "evaporates."

Though the bass line will, in most cases, continue to provide the foundation for an analysis of harmonic motion, you must be aware of possible changes from functional to non-functional patterning.

3. This item is often closely linked to the preceding: chordal and voice-leading ambiguity. The chord in bar 42 has at least two

123

possible interpretations—V$\frac{4}{2}$/F with D suspended (we expect resolution to E) or a G-minor triad with an added fourth (or persistent C pedal tone)—but an unhelpful bass change occurs in bar 44 and the chord itself disappears. Under these circumstances, how are we to read the voice-leading motion from D?

This is one of the most critical and most difficult problems of all, for the effect of composers' exploitation of ambiguity in chords is, of course, to open up a range of possible answers to the correct function of an individual sonority—and its members—in context. You should test alternatives in such situations, choosing the one that best fits into the larger context and emphasizing elements that do give some distinct directional tendency (here, the bass).

4. Following from the previous item, in passages where chords are uncertain, or chord movement non-functional or unusual, it is also likely that a secure interpretation of essential upper-voice patterns such as linear progressions will be very difficult to achieve. In this passage, for example, is a line C-D-E implied (literally, c''-d''-e)? A few factors argue in favor of it, but others—including register (often an important structuring device in Debussy)—argue against.

The patterns of the middleground or even "early foreground" are by no means so predictable as in traditional tonal music. The upper voice(s) in bars 40-43 trace a strong pattern of ascending fifths (with notes apparent in the obvious melodic motive): c''-g''-d'''', as the bass moves down in an equally directed whole-step pattern. Outside of the bass, there may be no immediate voice-leading or linear connection to bar 47.

5. Despite all, the traditional orienting function of the bass remains, if not entirely intact, still very powerful. Only in the radical "linear counterpoint" of the Twenties and in some "atonal" music is this function really compromised.

From the literature on Schenkerian analysis and twentieth-century music, we would recommend the following as beginning points for research:

1. Jonathan Dunsby and Arnold Whittall, *Music Analysis in Theory and Practice* , Chapter 5 (pp. 53-61).

2. Robert Morgan, "Dissonant Prolongations: Theoretical and Compositional Precedents," *Journal of Music Theory* 20 (1976), 49-91.

3. James Baker, "Schenkerian Analysis and Post-Tonal Music," in *Aspects of Schenkerian Theory*, pp. 153-186.

4. Joseph N. Straus, "The Problem of Prolongation in Post-Tonal Music," *Journal of Music Theory* 31/1 (1987): 1-21.

Also, see Christopher O. Lewis, "Into the Foothills: New Directions in Nineteenth-Century Analysis," *Music Theory Spectrum* 11/1 (1989): 15-23.

Exercises for Part II

EXERCISES IN FOREGROUND

A complete set of graphs is provided; add to them a second, more detailed foreground.

Assignment II.1
J. S. Bach, Invention in C Major (Ex. II.1). This reading, like those in Assignments II.2 and II.3, is reproduced from *The Book of the Musical Artwork*. Concentrate on introducing enough detail in foreground 2 to make the motives visible (perhaps by using an *Urlinietafel*-style representation, as in *Five Graphic Music Analyses*).

Assignment II.2
J. S. Bach, Invention in F Major (Ex. II.2). See the comments for Assignment II.1.

Assignment II.3
Schubert, "Heidenröslein" (Ex. II.3). See the comments for Assignment II.1.

Additional possibilities
The Book of the Musical Artwork contains more than fifty analysis graphs, the majority of which are in the format of Exs. II.1-II.3. Many of the graphs in *Structural Hearing* would benefit greatly in clarity from transcription to "standard" Schenkerian notation, with vertical alignment of the levels. One example: Figure 475 (Mozart, K. 280, II).

EXERCISES IN FOREGROUND AND MIDDLEGROUND

The background and first (or second) middleground for a composition are given; provide any remaining middlegrounds and the foreground. Assignment II.10 has separate instructions.

Assignment II.4
Chorale "Jesu, meine Freude" in J. S. Bach's setting. Use the analyzed bass from Assignment I.1; a combined graph of the background and middlegrounds 1 and 2 is given in Ex. II.4. Supply at least one more middleground and a foreground. As part of the exercise, you might also separate the levels shown in Ex. II.4 into separate graphs. A solution appears in the appendix.

Assignment II.5
Chorale "Wie schön leuchtet der Morgenstern" in J. S. Bach's setting. Use the analyzed bass from Assignment I.2; a graph of the background and middleground 1 is given in Ex. II.5. The graph lacks one element of middleground 1 which you should add: the initial ascent. Supply at least one more middleground and a foreground.

Assignment II.6
Chorale "Nun danket alle Gott" in J. S. Bach's setting. Use the analyzed bass from Assignment I.3; a graph of the background and middleground 1 is given in Ex. II.6.

Assignment II.7
Haydn, Sonata in C, Hob. XVI/1, Menuet (Exs. 1.5, 1.12, 4.1-4.5, II.7). A solution appears in the appendix.

Assignment II.8
C.P.E.Bach, Sonatine nuove, No. 4 (Ex. II.8). With the interruption and middleground fifth-line depending from $\hat{2}$, this sonatina has all the qualities of a sonata in miniature.

Assignment II.9
Schubert, Valses sentimentales, D. 779, no. 3 (Exs. 3.3 and II.9). Expect the left-hand afterbeats to duplicate some of the right-hand voice leading.

Assignment II.10
Schumann, "A Short Study," op. 68, no. 14. A shell for this analysis is given in Ex. II.10. Use your chordal reduction and your bass-line sketch from Assignment I.6 to complete the foreground. Add material as appropriate to the middleground 2 graph.

Additional possibilities

Free Composition actually contains *only* two "complete," three-level analyses: Figs. 22,b (Schumann, "Aus meinen Thränen spriessen"); and 49,2 (Brahms, Waltz, op. 39, No. 1). Thus, ample opportunity exists for you to complete analyses for which Schenker provides the framework or "clues." (Be sure to check all references first: Schenker mentions many compositions several times. Also check other texts, in particular *Structural Hearing*, Forte and Gilbert, and *The Book of the Musical Artwork*, to see if any of these contains completed analyses based on Schenker's readings.)

Some suggestions: Provide a foreground level for Fig. 30,a (Chopin, Mazurka, op. 17, no.3); or for Fig. 39,2 (Beethoven, op. 10, No. 3, II). Fig. 20,4 (Mozart, K. 331, II, Trio) is a (second) middleground graph; draw the background/first middleground content out of it and complete the set with a foreground graph. (As an additional exercise, merge Figs. 20,4 and 35,1.) Similar problems: Fig. 40,2 (Schubert); 40,7 (Chopin); 47,3 (Bach); 73,3 (Haydn); 76,4 (Bach); 76,5 (Chopin).

EXERCISES IN MIDDLEGROUND AND BACKGROUND

An analyzed bass and the first tone of the fundamental line are given; provide a complete set of graphs on that basis. Remember that some details of the notation of the analyzed bass may need to be changed in order to conform to the features of the principal upper part.

Assignment II.11

Chorale, "Ach, bleib bei uns, Herr Jesu Christ" in J. S. Bach's setting (Ex. II.11). No. 177 from the 371 Chorales. The fundamental line is from $\hat{3}$; e'' in bar 1 is a cover tone; there is no interruption.

Assignment II.12

Mozart, Symphony No. 35, III, Trio. The bass-line sketch appears in Ex. 1.11. The fundamental line is from $\hat{3}$, with interruption. Boundary play is an important feature.

Assignment II.13

Chopin, Mazurka, op. 67, No. 3 (Ex. II.12). The fundamental line is from $\hat{3}$ with interruption in the brief section B. Note but don't include the repetition in bars 17-32. (Use the form "bars 17-32 = 1-16.") A solution appears in the appendix.

EXERCISES IN FOREGROUND, MIDDLEGROUND AND BACKGROUND

Only the first tone of the fundamental line is given.

Assignment II.14

Purcell, Rondo (Ex. II.13). See the tonal outline in Ex. 3.6. The fundamental line is from $\hat{5}$.

Assignment II.15

Mozart, Symphony No. 36, Menuet and Trio. See Assignment I.8. Read both from $\hat{3}$ with an interruption in section B1.

Assignment II.16

Haydn, Symphony No. 100, II, Rondo theme. See Assignment I.4. Since this is the complete rondo theme, its background stands for the background structure of the whole movement. As an additional assignment, analyze the entire movement (three-part rondo with an extended coda). Read from $\hat{3}$ with an interruption.

Assignment II.17

Schubert, *Die schöne Müllerin*, "Morgengruß." See Assignment I.5. Read from $\hat{3}$ with an interruption.

THREE MORE ADVANCED EXERCISES (IN CHROMATICISM; SONATA FORM)

Assignment II.18

Liszt, Consolations, No. 1. Read from $\hat{5}$, without interruption. Score in Ex. II.14.

Assignment II.19

Schubert, "Daß sie hier gewesen!," op. 59, no. 2. Read from $\hat{3}$. A strophic song with three verses, each with a very extended prefix to the $\hat{3}$. The first two verses feature surface chromatic figures (mostly about ii), the final verse mode change and mixture as well. Before working out your analysis, read Carl Schachter's discussion of this song in "Motive and Text in Four Schubert Songs," in Beach, ed., *Aspects of Schenkerian Theory*, pp. 64-67. Score in Ex. II.15.

Assignment II.20

Use Schenker's graphs for the exposition and development of Beethoven, Piano Sonata, op. 10, no. 1, I, as the basis for a complete, multi-level analysis. *Free Composition*, Figs. 154,3; 154,7.

ESSAYS

Assignment II.21

Using Chapter 7 or an article in the published literature as your model, write an essay on concealed repetition in one of the Bach Inventions or Sinfonias. Alternate topics: Concealed repetition in one of the chorale preludes or a vocal work based on a chorale; concealed repetition and the sonata design in a movement from Haydn, Mozart, or Beethoven; motivic and voice-leading networks in a composition by Brahms (perhaps a piano composition from opp. 116-119 or a Lied from later opus numbers, such as op. 105).

Assignment II.22

Using Chapter 7 or an article in the published literature as your model, write an essay on chromaticism and formal design in an early nineteenth-century composition by Schubert, Mendelssohn, Liszt, or Chopin.

Assignment II.23

Using Carl Schachter's article "Motive and Text in Four Schubert Songs," in Beach, ed., *Aspects of Schenkerian Theory*, pp. 61-76, as your model, write an essay on the relationship between tonal structure and text setting in a Schubert song.

Assignment II.24

Write a critical essay comparing two (or more) published analyses of the same composition. Be sure to include your own analysis or detailed arguments in favor of one of the existing readings. If only one analysis is available in the literature, work out your own independently and base your essay on a defense of your reading.

Assignment II.25

Write an essay tracing the use of a particular sonority, technique, or pattern in a group of compositions. Some possibilities: the treatment of the subdominant [or other sonority] in [several] keyboard works by F. Couperin; chromatic descending lines from I to V in selected works by J. S. Bach (or C. P. E. Bach); the treatment of register (or the octave) in arias by Handel; tonal patterns in binary/ternary menuets by Mozart or Haydn; chromatic mediant progressions in Schubert waltzes; the triad as motive in Beethoven sonatas; orchestration as a clue to voice-leading structure or concealed repetition in works by Tchaikovsky or Brahms. Needless to say, it may be difficult to keep an essay of this kind within reasonable bounds. As possible models, see Roger Kamien, "Subtle Enharmonic Relationships in Mozart's Music," *Journal of Music Theory* 30/2 (1986): 169-183; and Ann K. McNamee, "The Role of the Piano Introduction in Schubert's *Lieder*," *Music Analysis* 4 (1985): 95-106.

EXAMPLE II.1 J.S.Bach, Invention in C Major

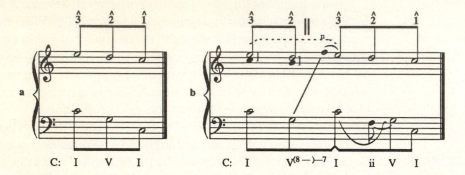

a.

C: I   V   I

b.

C: I   V^(8 —)—7   I   ii   V   I

a. Background: Space of a third.

b. Middleground 1: Interruption; lower thirds; expanded neighbor note.

c. Middleground 2: Initial ascent to $\hat{3}$; unfolding of the lower thirds; first-order lines; descending second in form of a seventh line (with counterpoint); bass couplings.

d. Foreground: Diminution; formal parallelism (① and ②); register transfers; second and third-order lines; arpeggiations.

c.

initial ascent   5th   7th   n   3rd

(unfoldings)   # ——— ♮

C: I   V   (8—)   —7   I   ii   V   I

mm.   1 2 3 4   5   6   7   8   9 10 11 12   13 14   15   16 17 18   19 20   21   22

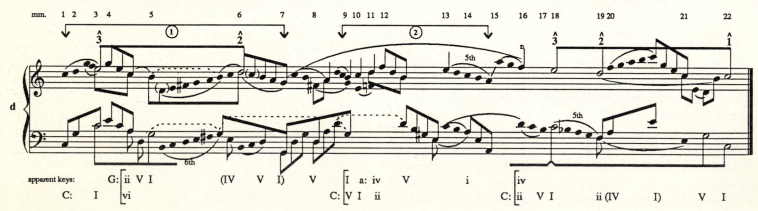

d.

① ②   5th   n   5th

6th   5th

apparent keys: G:[ii V I   (IV V I)   V   [I a: iv   V   i   [iv
C: I [vi   C:[V I ii   C:[ii V I   ii (IV   I)   V I

© 1988 Edwin Mellon Press. Reprinted by permission.

EXAMPLE II.1 continued

EXAMPLE II.2 J.S.Bach, Invention in F Major

a. Background: Space of a third.

b. Middleground 1: Interruption; neighbor note from V^{8-7}.

c. Middleground 2: First-order lines; register transfers; bass arpeggiations; secondary dominants.

d. Foreground: Diminution; lower-order lines; arpeggiations; unfoldings; ascending register transfers; parallel tenths; apparent keys; cadential dominant figure.

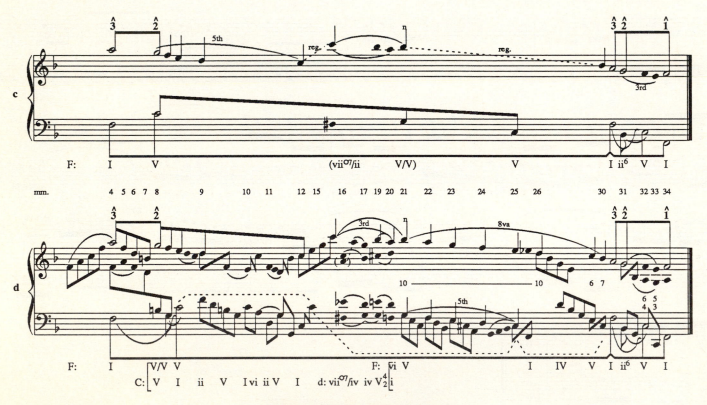

EXAMPLE II.2 continued

EXAMPLE II.3 Schubert, "Heidenröslein"

a. Background: Tonal space of the fifth.

b. Middleground 1: $I - IV^8 - V^{6-5} - I$.

c. Middleground 2: Initial ascent to $\hat{5}$; lines of the second order; descending register transfer (bass) with a dividing dominant.

d. Foreground: Diminution; lower-order lines; 3-4-4-3; ascending register transfers; downward arpeggiation; transformation of 8 to 10-6; cadential dominant; ii in appendix; cover tone G.

© 1988 Edwin Mellon Press.

Reprinted by permission.

EXAMPLE II.4 Chorale "Jesu, meine Freude" in J. S. Bach's setting, background/middleground //1 and 2

EXAMPLE II.5 Chorale "Wie schön leuchtet der Morgenstern" in J. S. Bach's setting, background/middleground 1

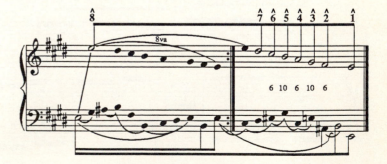

132

EXAMPLE II.3 continued

Lieblich

Sah ein Knab ein Rös- lein stehn, Rös- lein auf der Hei- den, war so jung und mor- gen- schön,

lief er schnell, es nah zu sehn, sah's mit vie- len Freu- den. Rös- lein, Rös- lein, Rös- lein rot,

wie oben

Rös- lein auf der Hei- den,

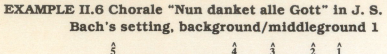

EXAMPLE II.6 Chorale "Nun danket alle Gott" in J. S. Bach's setting, background/middleground 1

EXAMPLE II.7 Haydn, Sonata in C, Hob. XVI/1, Menuet, background/ middleground 1

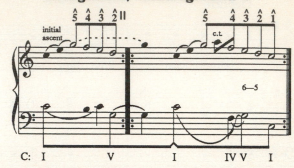

EXAMPLE II.9 Schubert, *Valses sentimentales*, D. 779, No. 3; background/middleground I

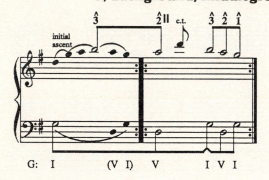

EXAMPLE II.11 Chorale, "Ach, bleib bei uns, Herr Jesu Christ" in J. S. Bach's setting; score and bass-line sketch

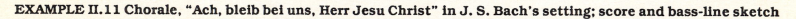

134

EXAMPLE II.8 C. P. E. Bach, Sonatine nuove, No. 4;
background/middleground //1 and 2 and score

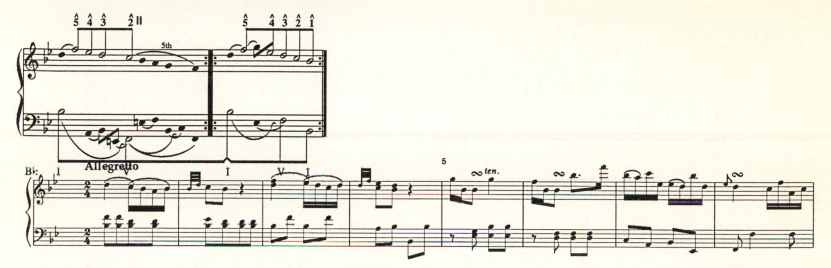

EXAMPLE II.10 Schumann, "A Short Study," op. 68, no. 14, shell for the analysis

EXAMPLE II.12 Chopin, Mazurka, op. 67, No. 3; score and bass-line sketch

mm.   5   8 13   16 33 40 41

EXAMPLE II.12 continued

EXAMPLE II.13 Purcell, Rondo

EXAMPLE II.14 Liszt, Consolations, No. 1

EXAMPLE II.15 Schubert, "Daß sie hier gewesen!", op. 59, no. 2

EXAMPLE II.15 continued

Bibliographical notes

I. GENERAL BIBLIOGRAPHY

The Schenker literature is already large and is constantly growing. Use the following publications by David Beach as general bibliographical resources.

1. "A Schenker Bibliography," *Journal of Music Theory* 13 (1969): 2-37 (reprinted in Maury Yeston, ed., *Readings in Schenker Analysis and Other Approaches* (New Haven 1977)).

2. "A Schenker Bibliography: 1969-1979," *Journal of Music Theory* 23 (1979): 275-286.

3. "The Current State of Schenkerian Research," *Acta Musicologica* 57/2 (1985): 276-307.

4. "Schenkerian Theory," *Music Theory Spectrum* 11/1 (1989): 3-14.

The bibliographies in these publications are thorough and reliable, but be warned that Beach's commentaries depart from the neutral, reportorial tone one might expect of a bibliographer; they show strong and obvious biases.

Also, see Larry Laskowski, *Heinrich Schenker: An Annotated Index to his Analyses of Musical Works* (New York 1978) for references in Schenker's published works to specific musical compositions.

II. AS BASIC REFERENCE TEXTS, USE THE FOLLOWING

1. Heinrich Schenker, *Free Composition*, ed. and trans. Ernst Oster, 2 vols. (New York 1979). Original German edition 1935.
   The fullest expression of Schenker's theories and the fundamental reference source for Schenkerian analysis.

2. _____, *Five Graphic Music Analyses* (New York 1969).
   The clearest models for complete sets of analytic graphs are to be found here.

3. Allen Forte and Steven Gilbert, *Introduction to Schenkerian Analysis* (New York 1983).
   With Salzer's *Structural Hearing* , this is the standard reference for pedagogical purposes, but it is also a complex book due to an attempt to combine traditional teaching of form genres with the study of Schenkerian analysis. Its strongest point is the careful introduction to foreground techniques in the first six chapters. Its weakest point is its reductive approach, which slights the early structural levels and the composing-out process.

4. Felix Salzer, *Structural Hearing*, 2 vols. (New York 1952; repr. ed. 1962).
   For many years the only textbook readily available to English readers, this is still excellent, though it is made difficult to use by the separation of text and musical examples into two volumes. Its strongest point is its clear presentation of concepts. The extension of Schenker's method to include music outside "Bach-to-Brahms" remains uniquely interesting. On the debit side, there is too much emphasis on harmonic aspects and a number of doubtful analyses.

5. Felix-Eberhard von Cube, tr. and ed. David Neumeyer, Scott Harris, and George R. Boyd, *The Book of the Musical Artwork* (Lewiston, NY 1988).
   This includes major portions of the *Lehrbuch der musikalischen Kunstgesetze* (unpublished manuscript, mostly written between 1934 and 1953). Its strongest points, for our purposes, are the concise tabular presentation of essential elements in Schenker's theory and the large number of complete sets of analytic graphs (more than in any other published source).

III. SELECTED ADDITIONAL WORKS BY SCHENKER OR HIS STUDENTS

1. Oswald Jonas, tr. John Rothgeb, *Introduction to the Theory of Heinrich Schenker* (New York 1982). Original German edition 1934.
   This is not always clear enough to serve effectively the function its title suggests, but it is definitely worthwhile reading if one already knows some Schenker.

2. *Music Forum.* A journal founded by Felix Salzer, published by Columbia University Press, and devoted to Schenkerian research.

3. Felix Salzer and Carl Schachter, *Counterpoint in Composition* (New York 1969).
   Still an excellent textbook for Schenker-oriented species counterpoint study. Later analysis chapters show the same weaknesses as *Structural Hearing.*

4. Heinrich Schenker, tr. E. M. Borgese, *Harmony* (Chicago 1954). Original German edition 1906.
   A speculative rather than practical harmony book which lays the foundation for Schenker's view of the tonal system. This is the first volume in a trilogy that continues with the *Counterpoint* and is completed with *Free Composition.* The translation lacks several extended passages from the original.

5. _____, tr. John Rothgeb, *Counterpoint*, 2 vols. New York: Longman, 1986. Original German editions, 1911, 1922.
   Extended and careful review of species counterpoint. For the serious student of Schenkerian theory, this is second in importance only to *Free Composition.*

6. _____, tr. Hedi Siegel, "A Contribution to the Study of Ornamentation," *Music Forum* IV (1976): 1-139.
   An early work.

7. _____, *Das Meisterwerk in der Musik*, 3 vols. (Munich: Drei Masken Verlag, 1925, 1926, 1930).

Essays translated in Kalib, Yeston, *Music Analysis,* and *Music Forum.* (See Beach's bibliographies for references to translations.)

IV. TWO ADDITIONAL SOURCES

1. David Beach, ed., *Aspects of Schenkerian Theory* (New Haven 1983).
   The studies in this collection cover a wide variety of topics and, although they grew out of a conference more than ten years ago, they still represent the preoccupations of many Schenkerian scholars today.

2. Maury Yeston, ed., *Readings in Schenker Analysis and Other Approaches* (New Haven 1977).
   An earlier essay collection similar to, but less comprehensive than, Beach *Aspects.* It includes, among other things, a translation of one of the most entertaining and penetrating of Schenker's polemical/analytical essays, "Organic Structure in Sonata Form," from the second volume of *Das Meisterwerk in der Musik.*

V. OTHER WORKS CITED

1. Edward Aldwell and Carl Schachter, *Harmony and Voice-Leading,* 2d. ed. (New York 1989).

2. Mary I. Arlin et al, *Music Sources,* 2d. ed. (Englewood Cliffs, NJ 1986).

3. James Baker, "Schenkerian Analysis and Post-Tonal Music," in *Aspects of Schenkerian Theory,* pp. 153-186.

4. Frederick Bashour, "A Model for the Analysis of Structural Levels and Tonal Movement in Compositions of the Fifteenth Century," 2 vols, Ph.D dissertation, Yale University, 1975.

5. David Beach, "Schenker's Theories: A Pedagogical View," in Beach, ed., *Aspects of Schenkerian Theory,* pp. 1-38.

6. David Beach, "The Fundamental Line from Scale Degree 8: Criteria for Evaluation," *Journal of Music Theory* 32/2 (1988): 271-294.

7. Peter Bergquist, "Mode and Polyphony around 1500," *Music Forum* 1 (1967): 99-161.

8. Wallace Berry, in *Form in Music*, 2d. ed. (Englewood Cliffs, NJ 1986).

9. Charles Burkhart, *Anthology for Musical Analysis*, 4th ed. (New York 1986).

10. Nicholas Cook, *A Guide to Musical Analysis* (New York 1987).

11. William Drabkin, "A Lesson in Analysis from Heinrich Schenker: The C Major Prelude from Bach's Well-Tempered Clavier, Book I," *Music Analysis* 4 (1985): 241-258.

12. Jonathan Dunsby and Arnold Whittall, *Music Analysis in Theory and Practice* (New Haven 1988).

13. Allen Forte, *Tonal Harmony in Concept and Practice*, third edition (New York 1979).

14. Robert Gauldin, *A Practical Approach to Eighteenth-Century Counterpoint* (Englewood Cliffs, NJ 1985).

15. Douglass M. Green, *Form in Tonal Music*, 2d. ed. (New York 1979).

16. Roger Kamien, "Subtle Enharmonic Relationships in Mozart's Music," *Journal of Music Theory* 30/2 (1986): 169-183.

17. Adele Katz, *Challenge to Musical Tradition* (New York 1945).

18. Stefan Kostka and Dorothy Payne, *Tonal Harmony*, 2d. ed. (New York 1989).

19. Leo Kraft, *Gradus* , 2d. ed. (New York 1987).

20. Joel Lester, *Harmony in Tonal Music*, 2 vols. (New York 1982).

21. Christopher O. Lewis, "Into the Foothills: New Directions in Nineteenth-Century Analysis," *Music Theory Spectrum* 11/1 (1989): 15-23.

22. Ann K. McNamee, "The Role of the Piano Introduction in Schubert's *Lieder*," *Music Analysis* 4 (1985): 95-106.

23. William J. Mitchell, "The Prologue to Orlando di Lasso's Prophetiae Sibyllarum," *Music Forum* 2 (1970): 264-273.

24. Robert Morgan, "Dissonant Prolongations: Theoretical and Compositional Precedents," *Journal of Music Theory* 20 (1976), pp. 49-91.

25. David Neumeyer, "The *Urlinie* from $\hat{8}$ as a Middleground Phenomenon," *In Theory Only* 9/5-6 (1987): 3-25.

26. David Neumeyer, "Fragile Octaves, Broken Lines: On Some Limitations in Schenkerian Theory and Practice," *In Theory Only* 11/3 (1989): 11-30.

27. Saul Novack, "The Analysis of Pre-Baroque Music," in *Aspects of Schenkerian Theory*, pp. 113-133.

28. Ernst Oster, "Re: A New Concept of Tonality (?)," *Journal of Music Theory* 4 (1960): 96-97.

29. Miguel Roig-Francoli, "Compositional theory and practice in mid-sixteenth century Castilian instrumental music: The *Arte de tañer fantasia* by Tomás de Santa María and the music of Antonio de Cabezón," Ph.D. dissertation, Indiana University, 1990.

30. Felix Salzer, "Heinrich Schenker and Historical Research: Monteverdi's Madrigal Oimè, se tanto amate," in *Aspects of Schenkerian Theory*, pp. 135-152.

31. Carl Schachter, "Motive and Text in Four Schubert Songs," in Beach, ed., *Aspects of Schenkerian Theory*, pp. 64-67.

32. Peter Spencer and Peter M. Temko, *A Practical Approach toThe*

Study of Form in Music (Englewood Cliffs, NJ 1988).

33. Joseph N. Straus, "The Problem of Prolongation in Post-Tonal Music," *Journal of Music Theory* 31/1 (1987): 1-21.

34. Susan Tepping, "Fugue Process and Tonal Structure in the String Quartets of Haydn, Mozart, and Beethoven," Ph.D. dissertation, Indiana University, 1987.

35. Roy Travis, "Toward a New Concept of Tonality," *Journal of Music Theory* 3/2 (1959): 257-284.

36. Nicol Viljoen, "Motivic Design and Tonal Structure in the Mazurkas of Frederic Chopin," Ph.D. dissertation, University of the OFS [South Africa], 1989.

37. Mary Wennerstrom, *Anthology of Musical Structure and Style* (Englewood Cliffs, NJ 1983).

38. Peter Westergaard, *Introduction to Tonal Theory* (New York 1975).

39. Allen Winold, *Harmony: Patterns and Principles*, 2 vols. (Englewood Cliffs, NJ 1986).

Solutions to Some Exercises

SOLUTION FOR ASSIGNMENT I.1 (BACH)

e: i   (ii°⁶V i)   (III i)   V (VI iv V) i   I ii⁶V I / III   i   V I / V i   ii°⁶V I

SOLUTION FOR ASSIGNMENT I.2 (BACH)

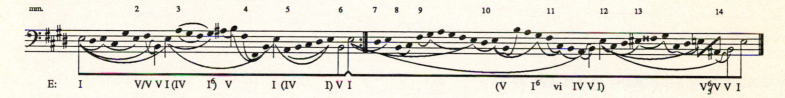

E: I   V/V V I(IV   I⁶) V   I (IV   I) V I   (V   I⁶ vi IV V I)   V⁶₃/V V I

SOLUTION FOR ASSIGNMENT I.9 (BRAHMS)

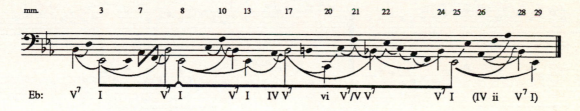

Eb: V⁷ I   V⁷ I   V⁷ I   IV V⁷   vi V⁷/V V⁷   V⁷ I   (IV ii V⁷ I)

SOLUTION FOR ASSIGNMENT II.4 (BACH)

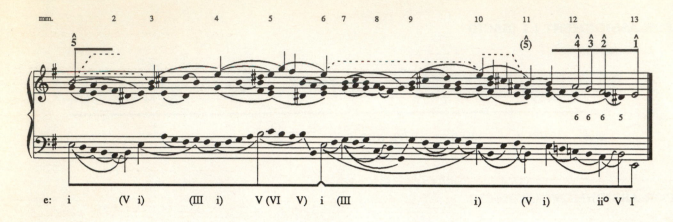

SOLUTION FOR ASSIGNMENT II.7 (HAYDN)

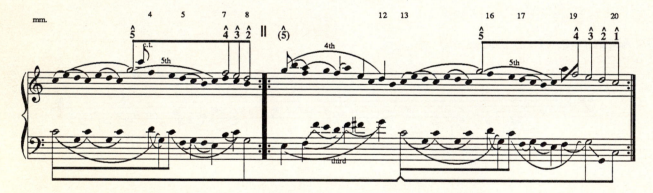

SOLUTION FOR ASSIGNMENT II.12 (CHOPIN)

Index